MAN
IN THE
MAKING

Other Books for Teens by Greg Johnson

If I Could Ask God One Question . . .
TYNDALE HOUSE PUBLISHERS

Life Is Like Driver's Ed.
VINE BOOKS

With Susie Shellenberger
258 Great Dates While You Wait
BROADMAN & HOLMAN PUBLISHERS

Opening Lines: 458 Discussion Starters
While You're on a Date
BROADMAN & HOLMAN PUBLISHERS

Getting Ready for the Guy/Girl Thing
REGAL BOOKS

What Hollywood Won't Tell You
About Sex, Love & Dating
REGAL BOOKS

Keeping Your Cool While Sharing Your Faith
TYNDALE HOUSE PUBLISHERS

Lockers, Lunchlines, Chemistry & Cliques:
77 Pretty Important Ideas on School Survival
BETHANY HOUSE PUBLISHERS

Cars, Curfews, Parties & Parents:
77 Pretty Important Ideas on Family Survival
BETHANY HOUSE PUBLISHERS

Camp, Carwashes, Heaven & Hell:
77 Pretty Important Ideas on Living God's Way
BETHANY HOUSE PUBLISHERS

Life, Love, Music & Money:
77 Pretty Important Ideas on Surviving Planet Earth
BETHANY HOUSE PUBLISHERS

With Michael Ross
Geek Proof Your Faith
ZONDERVAN PUBLISHING HOUSE

MAN IN THE MAKING

**What You Need To Know
As You're Becoming A Man**

GREG JOHNSON

BROADMAN
&HOLMAN
PUBLISHERS

Nashville, Tennessee

4253-95
0-8054-5395-4

Published by
Broadman & Holman Publishers, Nashville, Tennessee
Acquisitions and Development Editor: Janis Whipple
Page Design: Desktop Miracles, Addison, Texas
Cover Photo: Ron Chapple
Cover Design: Left Coast Design, Inc., Portland, Oregon

Dewey Decimal Classification: 305.23
Subject Heading: YOUNG MEN / CHRISTIAN LIFE
Library of Congress Card Catalog Number: 96-32722

Unless otherwise stated, all Scripture citation is from the New Living Bible, Tyndale House Publishers, 1996. Other passages are marked NASB the New American Standard Bible, © the Lockman Foundation, 1960, 1962, 1963, 1968, 1971, 1972, 1973, 1975, 1977, used by permission; NIV, the Holy Bible, New International Version, copyright © 1973, 1978, 1984 by International Bible Society; and NKJV, New King James Version, copyright © 1979, 1980, 1982, Thomas Nelson, Inc., Publishers.

Library of Congress Cataloging-in-Publication Data

Johnson, Greg.
    Man in the making : what you need to know as you're becoming a
man / Greg Johnson.
        p. cm.
    ISBN 0-8054-5395-4 (pbk.)
    1.Teenagers—Religious life. 2.Youth—Religious life.
3. Fathers and sons—Religious aspects—Christianity.
4. Christian life. I. Title.
BV4531.2.J594   1997
248.8'32—dc20   96-32722
                                                        CIP

97 98 99 00 01 1 2 3 4 5

To Troy and Drew,

May Christian manhood
be your greatest desire.

Contents

Foreword

Each year, I'm privileged to speak to tens of thousands of men—and a few teenage men—in the weekend seminars I lead throughout the country. In every city I'll have the chance to talk directly with dozens who open up about their lives.

Here's the good news: Men are finally getting serious about their relationship with God. They're pursuing Him like never before, and He's making the difference as they seek to become better husbands, fathers, and workers.

The not-so-good news is that a high percentage of men are still struggling in major areas: self-discipline, sexual thoughts, anger, bitterness. The reasons: they started out their younger years not pursuing, in many cases not even caring about, the high calling of Christian manhood. They thought they'd have time *later* to get things right.

It wasn't just "fun" they were after; it was escape from responsibility. They had an intense desire to stay in control of their own lives, so God never had the chance to do His work in them throughout the most significant years of their lives.

To the man, nearly every guy who struggles wishes he would have started out stronger. "I made some bad mistakes during my teenage years," is a line I hear all too often. Now they're facing the consequences. It's sad to see, mainly because, for most, it didn't have to be that way.

The real issue about becoming a man is character. It has more to do with what is on the inside than the outside.

I talk to men every weekend who are in their twenties, thirties, and forties who haven't grown up. They're boys trapped in the bodies of men. How can a forty-year-old man be referred to as a boy? A man is still a boy if he hasn't learned to grow up on the inside. It's possible to be a man and still be immature. But it is also possible to be a boy and put yourself on the fast-track of becoming a mature man.

That's what this book is all about. Greg Johnson knows teen guys. And he knows that many boys want to become men. But sometimes that process can get a bit confusing. When Greg was in his teen years, his dad wasn't around much, and he had some difficult moments in learning to become a man. He'd be the first to admit that pursuing Christian manhood wasn't even on his mind. Today, as a father of two boys, he's trying to be the coach to his sons that he never had.

Having a great coach can make all the difference in the world. In these pages, you're going to interact with a great coach. Greg's a great coach because he knows what it's like to play the game.

Do you want to become a man of character? Then you've picked up the right book. Greg will help you to not only become the man that you want to be, but the man that God wants you to be.

Steve Farrar
MEN'S LEADERSHIP MINISTRIES
AUTHOR OF *POINT MAN*

You're a Man in the Making!

What do you think it means to be a man? Here are a few yardsticks perhaps you've heard of:

★ Underarm hair

★ A deep voice

★ Shaving

★ A drivers license

★ Having sex with a girl

★ Graduating from high school

★ Partying

While a few may feel "manly" when they do these things, the measurement of manhood has nothing to do with age, body changes, or perceived adult privileges. Just the opposite is true. Manhood in no way consists of what's happening on the outside. Manhood begins—and ends—on the inside.

Throughout this book you'll be shown the difference between how a *boy* responds and how a *man* responds to the major issues in life. I've known a lot of males in their thirties and forties who still respond like boys. And my experience is that many boys have the ability and character to respond like men. But how do you know the difference?

I've chosen thirty-five areas boys must begin to track to determine their own progress toward Christian manhood. It's not the final word on what makes a man; it's just what I see as most of the top issues. While many of them seem to be challenging you on behavior-type issues (that is, what you're *doing*), don't miss the real point. *Christian manhood is an internal maturity issue.* It's the inside stuff. It's thinking like a man when your friends and the culture around you are "rewarding" you for acting like a boy.

Ever heard of the phrase "rite of passage"? It's an outward event that artificially promotes you to higher levels of maturity in the eyes of others. Most of the things mentioned at the beginning are considered "rites of passage." The belief is, if you can check one or more of these off of the list, you're a man.

God has a different list. It's a list based on *internal* qualities only He can build into your life.

You may be thinking that if you have to be perfect in thirty-five different areas, you'll never make it to manhood. Don't worry—just as God is patient with your progress, so must you be. He won't love you any more if you're succeeding in *every* area, and He won't love you any less if you don't have a clue. But be careful. His unconditional love and acceptance of you shouldn't put you to sleep as you move through your adolescent years toward adulthood. He wants *progress*. He wants you to attain true Christian manhood early in life so He can use you to greater degrees. God knows that you'll sense a pride you've never known when you not only *know* the right choices, but *make* them, as well (though feeling proud of your accomplishments isn't the goal). The world is in short supply of Christian men, and He'd like you to come through for the Kingdom. There are millions of Christian boys but few men.

If learning what it takes to become a Christian man is your goal, this book should help. One way to get the most out of these short challenges is to either read this book with Dad, or a man you respect and admire (if your dad isn't around). He'll be able to answer questions you'll have along the way. And he can give you immediate feedback on where you are. Maybe you're not as far away as you think.

Naturally, another great way to go through this book is on your own during a morning or evening devotional time. Don't hurry though. Let the challenge sink in. When you're done with each reading, take a minute to think how you're doing. Maybe even rate yourself from one to ten. The point is to discover where you are and then begin to take the action steps necessary to begin moving up the manhood ladder.

Dive in and have fun tracking your progress toward Christian manhood.

1

Picture Perfect

A friend of mine told me that his family used to be puzzle fanatics. "I don't know how we got into it," he said, "but when Dad would bring home those puzzles, everyone couldn't wait to open them up and get to them."

He remembers one time when he was fourteen that he played a practical joke on his family. His dad brought home three puzzles, all in the same size box. After he excused himself from dinner, and before everyone else was done, he sneaked downstairs, found a pair of scissors, cut the paper that sealed the bottom of each puzzle, and switched the lids!

"I told the rest of the family to hurry and come down so we could get started. I said that since they were only five hundred pieces each, we ought to do all three at once."

Like usual, they emptied all of the pieces out onto a card table, set the box up so they could see the picture while they were working on it, and began turning over the pieces.

"It took about an hour before my mom finally said, 'These pieces don't seem to match the picture.' That's when they all turned to look at me. I busted out laughing. I'd got 'em."

Along with teaching me a great joke (that you have my permission to try some time), my friend taught me something I hadn't thought about before: Nearly everyone I know is slowly trying to put the puzzle together of finding out who God really is. But many aren't looking at the right picture, and they're grabbing pieces from the wrong places.

When I was fifteen, my mom came into my room late one night after she'd had a huge fight with her second husband.

She said they just couldn't get along and were going to get a divorce. "But don't worry, Son," she said, "God will take care of us." When she said that, I told her, "Mom, there's no way there could be a God who would put us through this." It was then that I quit believing in God. The first divorce from my dad was bad enough, but now this second one after we'd established a measure of security again was too much for me to take. I took the pieces of my own pain and concluded God didn't exist.

Others take pieces from people or incidents in their lives and come to the same conclusions.

They've grabbed a piece from their grandma. "Though she's a nice old gal, she's not too cool. And she talks *way* too much about God." Unfortunately, her faith communicates that God is for old people who have no excitement in their life.

They've grabbed a piece from their science teacher who says, "God is for weak people who are afraid to use their minds."

They've grabbed a piece from the newspaper reports that another famous TV evangelist has been caught stealing money or spending a week with his secretary.

They've grabbed a piece from their local TV news program that shows the aftermath of a typhoon wiping out 50,000 people in India. "How could there be a God?" they reason. "Who would allow that many people to die?"

In their minds, these pieces of the "God puzzle" don't make a pretty picture. It looks nothing like someone you'd want to hang out with—let alone trust with your life today and eternity tomorrow.

What's the problem?

Like me at fifteen, they're not looking at the right picture!

When you're looking at the correct picture of God, you know right away that when you pick up a wrong piece that doesn't match the picture, that piece should immediately be discarded.

What *is* the right picture of God?

Three years later in my first year of college I found out it is Jesus Christ.

It's not a grandma, a stiff-haired evangelist you wouldn't buy a used car from, a painful incident, or a science teacher's put-downs of "weakling Christians." Jesus said, *"Anyone who has seen me has seen the Father!"* (John 14:9). You can't get any more obvious than that.

Do you have the wrong picture of God? You may if you find yourself not too motivated to spend any time with Him. And you definitely have the wrong picture if you believe He'll ruin your social life.

The only way to have the picture on the box match the pieces is to look at the life of Jesus. Before you ever consider giving up on God, make sure you've taken a long look at the life of Jesus as found in the four Gospels: Matthew, Mark, Luke, and John. There's no way to mistake what God looks like by examining closely the life, teachings, and work of the One we call "the Savior."

ULTIMATE CHOICE

"Am I going to learn about the right picture of Jesus from the Bible, or will I allow myself to get bits and pieces of the wrong God from the wrong places?"

BOYS. . .

. . . don't bother putting the right pieces together so they don't have to think about the right God.

MEN . . .

. . . look to the Bible and Jesus Christ for their picture of who God is.

THE WORD

The Son reflects God's own glory, and everything about him represents God exactly.

HEBREWS 1:3A

"The Father and I are one."

JOHN 10:30

ACTION IDEA

Put yourself on a sixty-day reading plan that will take you through Matthew, Mark, Luke, and John. Get to know Jesus Christ firsthand and decide for yourself.

2

How to Always Win

When you're in the heat of competition, are you the type who might "rub it in" if you are winning? Would you stare down an opponent after you just burned him for a lay-in or touchdown? Are you so intent on getting the victory that you think losing is the worst thing?

The popularity of ESPN has moved sports to a whole new level in many homes. With the other junk on TV, many families tune in only to sports. They play sports, too—every sport, every season. The drive to compete is fierce, and the emphasis on winning—and putting your opponent in the ground—often takes the fun out of competition. After all, winning means you're a winner, losing means you're a loser, right?

A number of years ago, when I was editor of *Breakaway* magazine, I had the chance to play NBA All-Star Kevin Johnson of the Phoenix Suns one-on-one (as part of a story, of course). It was a 100-degree day in Kevin's hometown of Sacramento, and the outdoor court was your typical playground variety. He was in his prime, I was . . . well past mine. Before we began, I told him how bad my ankles were, how I'd just come off an injury, and was out of shape. Then I went through the rules. "To 15 by ones, alternating possessions instead of make-it-take-it. That's the only chance I'll have at winning."

He then said three words to me I'll never forget. "You already won."

I didn't have to think about his statement long to know what he meant. Simply having the chance to use my arms, legs,

4

and ankles (what was left of them) was a victory. Playing against an NBA All-Star was a happy ending in itself.

He was right. I had a grin on my face the whole game. When he swished twenty-five-footers over my meager defense, or when he blew by and dunked on me four times (including an incredible reverse dunk you had to see to believe), I was smiling. The score was 15-7 (he let me shoot from the outside—luckily I was hitting), but I truly *was* the winner.

I've competed in nearly every sport: baseball, football, soccer, wrestling, track, softball, golf, and of course hundreds of games of basketball. I like to win, but what I've learned is that simply playing and competing is the true victory. I only remember the final score of one game I ever played: My high school team lost 57-52 in the state championship game. But you know, at least I got to start in a state championship game at a pro basketball arena—thousands of other Oregon boys never even made it to the tournament.

When I was a boy, I didn't understand that you were victorious if you just had the chance to play. I thought you were a loser if you came out on the short end of the score. I was wrong.

If you're an athlete, or you just like to compete to win, be careful. ESPN shows us there are a lot of big boys running up and down the court or the field who haven't learned to be men. They talk trash, they argue when they don't get their way, they swear, fight, yell at their teammates—they'll do anything to win and look good.

As editor of *Breakaway*, I interviewed more than thirty Christian professional athletes, and every one of them liked to win more than lose. And nearly all agreed that if Jesus was competing, He would have done everything within the rules to win. But when the contest was over, He'd recognize it for what it is: Athletic talents are part of God's gifts given to be enjoyed on earth. He knows that the T-shirt is wrong when it says, "Basketball Is Life." Loving God and loving your neighbor as yourself is where true life is found.

Yes, winning is important, but a Christian *man* should be able to look up at the scoreboard after *any* game and say in his heart, "I competed. I did the best I could. I won."

ULTIMATE CHOICE

"Will I realize that competing and doing my best is the ultimate victory, or will I show by my actions and attitudes that competition isn't any fun unless I can chalk up another victory?"

BOYS . . .

. . . see themselves as losers if they lose, and can't see themselves as winners unless they win.

MEN . . .

. . . know there are lessons to be learned from losing, but the greatest lesson in competition is simply having the chance to play.

THE WORD

Remember that in a race everyone runs, but only one person gets the prize. You also must run in such a way that you will win. All athletes practice strict self-control. They do it to win a prize that will fade away, but we do it for an eternal prize. So I run straight to the goal with purpose in every step. I am not like a boxer who misses his punches. I discipline my body like an athlete, training it to do what it should. Otherwise, I fear that after preaching to others I myself might be disqualified.

1 CORINTHIANS 9:24–27

I strain to reach the end of the race and receive the prize for which God, through Christ Jesus, is calling us up to heaven.

PHILIPPIANS 3:14

ACTION IDEA

Think of the last few games you've competed in. How could a more positive attitude about simply playing the game have helped improve your performance and enjoyment of the competition?

3 Growing in Friendship with Dad

et's admit the obvious: While you're under your parents' roof, someone's the boss—usually Dad. Though Dad finds creative ways to show his love to his son, he must also wear the black hat. That means almost weekly, he's the "bad guy." He sets curfew rules, social limits, allocates allowances, barks out chore schedules, reminds you of homework, and since you're one of the guys of the house, he probably expects you to set an example for everyone else.

While some guys resent Dad's authority, if it's balanced with love, most learn to live with it. When it's time to leave home, they know the rules will change. And so does their relationship with him.

How do you want that relationship to be when you *visit* home instead of *live* there? Will your relationship be tense or will you develop into good friends? Believe it or not, how you relate to him during your teenage years may determine how good friends you'll be for the next thirty years!

Before I throw a few ideas at you on how to cultivate a friendship with Dad, let me make what might be a big assumption: Your dad wants to be a good friend to you—not only now, but for the rest of your life! While not every home has a dad—or a good dad—most do.

With that in mind, put into practice a few of these extra tips. After all, what do you want most? To get your way a few more times the next four to six years, or to have a good friend for life?

Pray for him. Don't just pray silently before you head off into dreamland, but out loud *with* him. Start by asking God to give him wisdom and courage in decision making, a productive day on the job, a close relationship with God, and good health. Initiate prayer with him. Tell him your needs as well. The more you both can understand each other now—while praying for God's best—the more you'll learn to trust each other when potential sources of conflict arise.

Don't try to manipulate him. When you were little, you probably whined and pouted until you got your way. Now that you're older, the more you use "the silent treatment"—door slams, half-truths, and other forms of manipulation to get your own way—the more he'll have to play the bad guy.

Try this: obedience first, negotiate second. That is, do what he tells you, then later, in a calm tone, logically discuss what might have been a good alternative. Your goal shouldn't be to win the argument (a definite bad goal!), but to influence his future decisions based on your growing maturity. It's kind of like a coach who "discusses" a bad call with a referee. He's not trying to get the ref to change the call (since that's impossible), he's trying to get the *next* call.

Calm discussion shows maturity. Manipulation or arguing tells him you've just sophisticated your whining and pouting from your grade-school years.

Ask his opinion and ask questions. Dads love it when they can be a voice in their sons' decisions! Does this mean you're locked into following all of his advice? No. But usually, the perspective his experience can give will be the major piece to getting the right answer.

Spend time with him on one of his hobbies. Your dad has likely already developed a few hobbies that he'll be doing the rest of his life: golf, gardening, tennis, computers, etc. Try plugging into one of those so you'll always have something in common.

Watch him like a hawk. There are certain things your dad does that are really good: how he treats your mom, his patience with your little brother, being a safe driver, not watching too much TV, working hard, being responsible. Well, OK, maybe he's not batting 1.000, but it *is* possible he does have a few worthwhile qualities.

It's also possible he has a few that aren't that hot, too. Take the good stuff and leave behind the bad. You know the difference, and if you don't, ask your dad what good things he'd like you to copy, and what not-so-good ones he'd like you to learn from. He'll tell you!

Pray, obey, ask, do, and watch. Not the typical formula for developing a lifelong friendship, but a pretty good start toward moving to the next stage in your relationship with the dad in your life.

ULTIMATE CHOICE

"Will I choose to keep the bigger goal of becoming friends with my dad, or the smaller goal of learning the tricks to get my own way?"

BOYS . . .

. . . try to manipulate their fathers to achieve the short-term goal of getting what they think they need.

MEN . . .

. . . know the importance of a lifelong friendship with their father and make persistent attempts to build their relationship with him. They know that God chooses to use their dad to mold their life and make it everything it was intended to be.

THE WORD

A wise son brings joy to his father, but a foolish son grief to his mother.

PROVERBS 10:1, NIV

"See, I will send you the prophet Elijah before that great and dreadful day of the LORD comes. He will turn the hearts of fathers to their children, and the hearts of children to their fathers; or else I will come and strike the land with a curse."

MALACHI 4:5–6

Talk to your dad about setting a consistent time that you two can be together—a Saturday morning breakfast, Wednesday evening at McDonald's, a Sunday afternoon hike. You don't need to have an agenda, but it could turn out to be the highlight of your week.

4 Spiritual Buffness— The Choice Is Yours

If you had to choose between a buff bod or a flabby one, which would you select? Though most guys would love to be well-built and muscular, looking like John Jacobs of the Power Team, it doesn't happen overnight.

If you could be a shallow Christian or one with depth, which would you go for? Again, tough choice. Shallow is easy; depth takes effort.

Let's examine three different types of Christians.

First, the flabby, shallow Christian simply hides his Bible, purchases a wardrobe of "couch potato" T-shirts and then lives up to what's written on his chest. His favorite book is *A Lazy Man's Path to Heaven*. And since this fellow knows God is forgiving, and since he's *accepted-Jesus-Christ-as-his-personal-Lord-and-Savior,* his ticket is paid. Why waste energy being someone he really doesn't want to be?

Second, there's the person who really wants to be buff and have some depth as a follower of Christ but is unknowingly living off vitamins instead of meat. The logic is that vitamins are easier to take, plus they make big *promises* about how much they help.

What are the vitamins?

⭐ DC Talk tapes

⭐ *Breakaway* magazine

⭐ This book!

11

Do you grasp the concept? Christian magazines, books, music, TV, videos, or movies are only supplements. Real faith needs nourishment by meat! Reading, listening, or watching Christian "things" doesn't do it alone. In fact, if taken without meat, they work more like diet pills that make you "feel full" but provide no real nourishment.

The third type of Christian is the person who uses the Bible as his *main source* for spiritual buffness. Only the depth of God's Word gives the depth of spirit that you and others can draw from. Resources like Christian music and magazines can then *add* to a faith already being nourished.

This month, try something radical. *Don't* listen to a Christian tape or pick up a Christian magazine until you've opened The Book first. (Most *adults* aren't even this radical!) God's Word may not feel as exciting as a music video, but it provides a hundred times more depth!

ULTIMATE CHOICE

"Will I try to attain spiritual muscle through 'diet pills' that were only meant to be supplements, or will I allow the meat of God's Word to build me up?"

BOYS . . .

. . . don't realize that "spiritual supplements" can't build muscle, and since they are often more visually pleasing, they pursue them first.

MEN . . .

. . . know the difference between pumping iron and lifting fluff. They know that having God talk with them through the pages of His Word is what can put on the spiritual muscles necessary to be the man of God they want to be.

THE WORD

All Scripture is inspired by God and is useful to teach us what is true and to make us realize what is wrong in our lives. It straightens us out and teaches us to do what is right. It is God's way of preparing us in every way, fully equipped for every good thing God wants us to do.

2 TIMOTHY 3:16–17

Such things were written in the Scriptures long ago to teach us. They give us hope and encouragement as we wait patiently for God's promises.

ROMANS 15:4

ACTION IDEA

In the last week, estimate the amount of time (in minutes) you've spent with these things:

★ Reading Christian magazines: _____

★ Listening to Christian music: _____

★ Reading Christian books: _____

★ Reading the Bible and praying: _____

5 *Loosening the Peer Pressure Valve*

Picture what occurs at nearly every school in America:

Eighth-grader Bobby Joe Billings is minding his own business walking by the track on his way to class. Buff Studley (one of the cool ninth-graders) stops him and asks if Bobby Joe likes to party.

When Bobby Joe thinks about parties, he imagines a group of guys getting together to eat pizza, watch scary movies, play Sega, drink pop, and maybe make a few anonymous phone calls to girls they could never talk to at school.

Buff, of course, is talking about drinking.

Though semi-naive, Bobby Joe quickly realizes he's being invited to a party with the cool group (which means doing what the group thinks is cool—drinking). "I love to party!" he says with excitement. Buff gives him the details.

As he walks to his first period class, Bobby Joe wears a smile. Reality hits moments later when he suddenly feels queasy.

What Bobby Joe has just done is give in to peer pressure. He wasn't trying to; it just happened. Now he is faced with a tougher choice. Does he go to the party and perhaps be tempted to do something he'll regret, or does he try to back out gracefully? Tough consequences either way. To get permission to go to the party, he'll probably have to lie. If he's caught, he'll be grounded until age thirty-two! If he backs out, he risks losing ground in the battle to join the cool group. If you've been paying attention, you've realized Bobby Joe's problem is more than peer pressure. What he really wants is to *be* someone else (not *do* something right or wrong). So he lied to Buff. He concealed his real character in a split second—all with the hope of being liked by a group he thinks has more going for it than his current one.

Whether we directly go into what we know to be wrong (cheating, stealing, swearing, drinking, drugs, or sex), or we only dabble in the "questionables" (staying out late, ignoring someone else who's cheating off your paper, being with someone who's stealing), it's never someone else who actually makes us do it. We make the choice.

Our hope, of course, is to have more and "better" friends. Believe it or not, this often works. If it didn't, people wouldn't try it! Everyone, whether six or sixty, is tempted to "bend" in order for someone to like him. In the teenage years, the pressure is at its worst. It's the hungry urge to do what others are doing to fit in. Sometimes we think the only way to get friends is to lie about who we really are.

What does God think about peer pressure? Though He says, "Don't copy the behavior and customs of this world," He wants you to allow Him "to transform you into a new person by changing the way you think" (Romans 12:2).

Let's assume for a minute that, deep within you, you really do want to please God. Though you don't know everything about Him yet, you feel like He probably has a few more answers on life than Buff Studley. If you were to hang around for very long with someone like Buff, you would become like him. You would act like him, think like him, maybe even begin to talk like him.

It's God's plan that we move toward the goal of becoming more like His Son, Jesus Christ. This is a big goal; that's why God gave us a lifetime to work on it!

Will becoming more like Christ get you many friends in school? Not always. It depends on what type of friend you want. And it depends on what type of person you want to be in the future. Remember, your teenage years don't last that long. To be like Buff, are you willing to throw right and wrong out the door?

Learning to become more like Christ, however, means you have to spend time with Him. God knows the pressure is on. He doesn't want to sit idly by, hoping you'll have the strength to withstand. He wants to provide the inner muscle it takes to combat the outer pressure you feel. One way to get that inner muscle is to mine the treasures of God's Word. But to find any worthwhile treasure, you have to dig for it!

Remember when your dad taught you how to start a lawnmower? He didn't just *tell* you how to do it, he *showed* you. The actions and words of Jesus and others in the Bible can give you the tools to do what's right.

Whatever you find when you read, whether a verse that would be good to memorize or a specific person who courageously stood for what he believed, make an attempt at writing it down. It will help you realize you found something.

ULTIMATE CHOICE

"When the pressure is on from other guys at school, will I forget who I want to be and follow along, or will I make decisions based on who I am, instead of who I *think* I want to be?"

BOYS . . .

. . . shoot for the low-end goal of allowing friendship with the cool group to determine what they act like.

MEN . . .

. . . realize the pressure to be someone else—to please someone else—is always there. They make choices based on the person they want to become, not what others want them to do.

THE WORD

Don't copy the behavior and customs of this world, but let God transform you into a new person by changing the way you think. Then you will know what God wants you to do, and you will know how good and pleasing and perfect his will really is.

ROMANS 12:2

> *Stop loving this evil world and all that it offers you, for when you love the world, you show that you do not have the love of the Father in you. For the world offers only the lust for physical pleasure, the lust for everything we see, and pride in our possessions. These are not from the Father. They are from this evil world. And this world is fading away, along with everything it craves. But if you do the will of God, you will live forever.*
>
> 1 JOHN 2:15–17

ACTION IDEA

Ask three trusted friends a serious question: "Do you think I'm too much of a follower around friends at school?"

Take two minutes and think about your actions from the last few days. How much of what you do and say is because you get attention or praise from those you want to impress?

6

Souls Don't Have Color

I have a confession to make: Besides one African-American girl in my first grade class, I did not have another person of color in any of my classes—all the way through high school! I went to public school in a part of the Northwest where there were only white people. Though I remember my grandpa having some prejudiced tendencies, my dad didn't. Neither did I. There was no reason to treat anyone differently, because everyone of color whom I had contact with had been fair and normal around me.

But I did learn to fear, a bit, what I didn't know. Television did that, I think. The stereotype of black males in particular made me unconsciously keep my distance. When college hit, however, I wanted to have friends of color. I took advantage of every opportunity to hang out and play basketball with whoever was there, no matter what their skin looked like. Even with this desire to expand my friendships, I had a fear of not being accepted, liked, or included. It sometimes made me hold my distance.

I've learned through the years that race is the type of issue where you pretty much believe what your family has taught you. Not always, of course, just mostly. So what have we been taught? Sadly, many have learned to distrust other races. Some believe, "They have their ways, we have ours. Why upset the apple cart and try to change things?" Others have been taught to hate based solely on color. A few believe they're superior *because* of their color.

What does the Bible specifically say about how to relate to someone whose skin is a different shade than yours?

Nothing.

The reason is simple: God knows that souls don't have a color. While He cares about our life here on earth, He's much more concerned with our souls—the spirit within us that lives for eternity. If He drew attention to the differences in skin color among all of His creation, it would be like acknowledging differences in nose shape, height or weight, balding or hairy people—in short, stuff that simply doesn't make a difference in the grand scale of eternity.

By God's silence on these issues, it is easy to see how people look down on those who are different from them. While the past may have had other reasons, I truly think that when sinful men want to feel better about themselves because they do not know how to deal with their inadequacies, they create something to be lord over. Our ancestors (and even a few of our close relatives) have made skin color the way to determine whom they think is better. In a sad way, it's just like what grade schoolers do to each other on the playground. They ridicule the kid who can't throw a baseball, the girl who's a bit overweight, or the guy who's small and wears glasses. Why? So they can momentarily feel like they're better than someone else.

Pulling this grade school trick with an entire race, however, goes much deeper. It shows how ignorant and insecure a person actually is. And it shows a total lack of knowledge and appreciation for God's Word. John said it best: "If someone says, 'I love God,' but hates another Christian, that person is a liar; for if we don't love people we can see, how can we love God, whom we have not seen? And God himself has commanded that we must love not only him but our Christian brothers and sisters, too" (1 John 4:20–21).

This passage makes it clear we are to take people one at a time. Yes, it says "hates another Christian," but there are millions of Christians who wear a variety of skin colors. An entire race cannot ever be judged. You judge people one at a time, whether their skin is white, black, brown, yellow, red, or plaid.

Once the biblical issue of loving our neighbor as our-selves is settled, the next logical question is "Why?" Why should I, a white male, seek to have the knowledge and skills necessary to relate to people of any color but my own?

Along with the Scripture's command above (among dozens that talk about loving others), and the example of how Jesus dealt with people from every part of Israel, God may want to use me to reach them for the Kingdom or to minister the life of Jesus to another brother or sister in Christ. Paul said it best: "So everywhere we go, we tell everyone about Christ. We warn them and teach them with all the wisdom God has given us, for we want to present them to God, perfect in their relationship to Christ. I work very hard at this, as I depend on Christ's mighty power that works within me" (Colossians 1:28–29). Paul doesn't qualify his remark with comment on skin color.

If you don't know how to relate to someone outwardly "different" than you, how do you get to know him better? This is what I did:

⭐ When I met a guy whom I wanted to get to know, I first found something we had in common and spent time with him. That is, I built a normal friendship like I would with anyone else.

⭐ Once that relationship was built, and when it was appropriate, I talked about my fears and my own back-ground. Honesty worked. My first black friend and I talked through my questions. Since he was used to liv-ing in a white man's world, I wanted to know what his past had been like; what acts of prejudice he'd experi-enced; what his family taught him about white people. And how I could overcome my subtle fears of other black men. It was a tough conversation. But I learned more from that hour about what it was like to walk in his shoes than a dozen textbooks could have taught me.

⭐ I learned to never back away from another person because of his color. Since I wouldn't have ever con-sidered keeping my distance from someone because of their height, weight, or shoe size, I decided it was pretty dumb to do it because of color. If you were sheltered like I was, it may take a bit more effort, but it will *always* be worth the risk.

★ I removed everything from my vocabulary that had any negative racial overtones. I figured that if I truly wanted to be color-blind, I'd learn to believe it better by speaking the truth. Plus, I refused to even listen to someone who was talking negatively solely based on race. I'd walk away. And if it was a friend who was making racial comments or "jokes," I'd take him aside, in private, and tell him it wasn't appreciated.

I hope you're not growing up as sheltered as I was. If you are, you likely can't help it—you have to live where your family lives. But one day, you'll be able to make conscious choices to break out of your comfort zones. I've made that choice now dozens of times in my life, and I know I'm a richer man. Learning—and believing—that souls do not have color has also given me a clearer glimpse of how God looks at all of His creation. The view is good.

ULTIMATE CHOICE

"Will I believe there are differences between the races and keep myself away from others, or will I see with God's eyes that a man's soul does not have a color attached to it?"

BOYS . . .

. . . allow family prejudices and their own fears to keep them away from those who look different than themselves.

MEN . . .

. . . know that to love all men the way Jesus did they must break through their own fears and embrace friendships with people of every race.

THE WORD

And now I want to urge you, . . . that we should love one another. This is not a new commandment,

*but one we had from the beginning. Love means
doing what God has commanded us, and he has
commanded us to love one another, just as you
heard from the beginning.*

2 JOHN 1:5

*"So now I am giving you a new command-
ment: Love each other. Just as I have loved you, you
should love each other. Your love for one another
will prove to the world that you are my disciples."*

JOHN 13:34–35

ACTION IDEA

What keeps you from building more friendships with
other people of color? Is there one person you can begin to
spend time with? What can you do this week to start—or
continue—this important process?

7   *The Male Disease*

As a seventeen-year-old, Henry hadn't been driving too long when he faced a split-second decision. An older man cut Henry off as he tried to enter the freeway. It made young Henry hopping mad! He pulled up next to the man, gave him an angry look, drove in front of him, and slowed down. The old man darted over and around and did the same. Henry tailgated for a mile or so, and then the man pulled over. Delighted that he'd "won," Henry didn't leave it be. Instead, he parked behind the old guy to get out and give him a piece of his mind. After a brief exchange of words, Henry punched the man. The man reached under his seat, pulled out a .357 and fired one shot into Henry's chest.

On the side of the highway this young high school graduate died. He was a church-going kid that everyone said had so much to live for. The old man was acquitted.

What killed Henry wasn't a gun. It was his male pride. A pride that led to anger, a couple of poor choices, and two parents who will never see a son experience all that life could have offered.

There are two types of pride. The first is a *good pride*. You feel it when

    ☆ you score the winning goal for your hockey team;

    ☆ your sister sets a school record in her SAT scores;

    ☆ your dad meets the President of the United States;

> ✶ America does something cool the whole world says was good;
>
> ✶ your school wins the state football championship.

Then there's a *bad pride*. It rears an ugly head when

> ✶ someone cuts you off on the freeway;
>
> ✶ another guy at school points out to everyone in class the D- you received on the spelling test that only contained words with three letters in them;
>
> ✶ you throw a fit because you just lost to your little brother in Monopoly for the tenth straight time;
>
> ✶ you say something mean to your girlfriend, but instead of apologizing, you make a joke about it, deny you really meant it, or accuse *her* of being overly sensitive.

Males aren't the only people who let their pride get in the way of doing the right thing (or *not* doing the wrong thing), but it's primarily a man disease. We hate it when our ego is bruised, when someone gets the better of us, or when we're made to feel stupid. To a small degree we sometimes can't help it; God put us together with a strong pride. But we *can* (1) recognize the potential dangers of our pride and (2) try to give it back to God.

Let's talk danger first. How can our pride put us in harm's way? Taking a look at what the Bible says is the best place to start.

"Pride leads to arguments" (Proverbs 13:10). How many males have let their pride push them toward a war of words? And how many times has that verbal volley led to something more serious—like fist fights, weapons, and worse? The results: broken teeth, broken bodies, perhaps jail, and a lifetime of regret.

"Pride leads to disgrace, but with humility comes wisdom" (Proverbs 11:2). Have you ever noticed what can disgrace a professional athlete? A temper-tantrum on national TV. A drug

or drinking problem (which can be an inability to cope with having your pride bruised). Cheating in competition, or trying to gain an unfair advantage (steroids, sucker-punching an opponent while the ref isn't looking). The results: You wear a label (cry baby, cheater) your entire life.

"The LORD despises pride; be assured that the proud will be punished" (Proverbs 16:5). God can't live with a child who allows his pride to give His name a bad reputation. God still loves His proud child, but He will use His power to bring him low until his child understands the value of keeping it in check. The result: God promises to keep His distance. "Though the LORD is great, he cares for the humble, but he keeps his distance from the proud" (Psalm 138:6).

"Pride goes before destruction, and haughtiness before a fall" (Proverbs 16:18). Some men's pride will not allow them to turn to God—for their entire lifetimes! The result: Spiritual destruction is their chosen end.

"Love is patient and kind. Love is not jealous or boastful or proud or rude" (1 Corinthians 13:4). Where pride dwells, love cannot. The result: Those filled with unchecked pride can't love as they should or receive love that they could.

Once we've recognized the dangers of "bad pride," we must give it back to God. How do we do that?

Just as we trust God's power and love to forgive our sins, and as we show our trust in His faithfulness when we pray, God is good at taking care of things when they are in His hands. It isn't easy to trust God with the bad pride that can get us into so much trouble, but it can be done. Think of how "unnatural" it is to feel forgiven just by asking for it from a God you've never seen. And it's "unnatural" to pray to Him about all that weighs on our heart. Yet we cannot deny we feel a peace when requests we've offered are truly put in His capable hands.

If we tell God to take the feelings of bad pride that creep in, He can be trusted to do so. And when you do this, it's good to ask Him to replace it with something. Humility would be the obvious choice. When we ask for humility, we're not asking to be turned into a wimp; we're not asking to be shown a way to chicken out—we're asking to be like Jesus. There was nothing wimpy about Jesus when He chose to ignore the insults from those whom *He* created. Jesus didn't chicken out when He willingly died for the proud hearts of mankind so they could have access to God and heaven. He chose the high road.

You and I know that it's easy, almost natural, to vent when the swollen rivers of pride want to overflow. It takes a man, however, to give God your pride and ask for humility. When you're able to do that, God gives you the power to act in the same way as Jesus.

If Henry would have dropped his pride and asked God for humility, instead of allowing it to overflow, he would likely still be around today.

ULTIMATE CHOICE

"Will I allow the bad pride to consume my thoughts, or will I turn it over to Jesus and ask Him to give me the power to take the high road of humility?"

BOYS . . .

. . . fail to recognize the destructive power of their pride, and seem to always be facing consequences because of it.

MEN . . .

. . . readily admit the power of pride, but they admit it to God, asking Him to replace it with the humility—and power— of Jesus.

THE WORD

He has performed mighty deeds with his arm; he has scattered those who are proud in their inmost thoughts.

LUKE 1:51, NIV

Since God chose you to be the holy people whom he loves, you must clothe yourselves with tenderhearted mercy, kindness, humility, gentleness, and patience.

COLOSSIANS 3:12

> *You younger men, accept the authority of the elders. And all of you, serve each other in humility, for "God sets himself against the proud, but he shows favor to the humble." So humble yourselves under the mighty power of God, and in his good time he will honor you.*
>
> 1 PETER 5:5–6

ACTION IDEA

What makes your pride burst out to the surface for all to see? Begin to ask God to help you recognize when the bad pride hits, and pray that you'll have the true strength to ask for humility when it does.

8   *Born Winners*

Grab a pencil and finish each of the sentences below:

★ My mom thinks I'm . . . _____

★ I feel really successful when . . . _____

★ My brother/sister would say I'm . . . _____

★ I felt really good about myself when . . . _____

_____

★ My dad thinks I'm . . . _____

★ People who know me say I'm . . . _____

★ I'm really good at . . . _____

★ God thinks I'm . . . _____

As the portrait of your life is being painted, you are influenced by the brush strokes from a variety of people in your life. For most guys, their parents, siblings, and friends seem to use the thickest paint. That is, what others think or say about you often determines how good or bad you feel about yourself. When you're shown love and are told the truth about your character and abilities, the picture looks good. If you're constantly getting put down or neglected, you'll likely feel your picture looks like an anorexic stick figure.

What makes the difference?

Truth.

When you are told the truth about who you are, your portrait begins to look more like a Rembrandt. (He was a famous painter a few hundred years ago, known for his incredible portraits of people.) When I was in high school, I got by on "half-truths," and the consequences—had I not heard *the* truth— could have been devastating.

By the time my senior year rolled around, I *thought* I had a lot going for me. I was semi-popular because I was on the varsity basketball team—people told me I had some talent. I had a small group of friends I'd party with—they told me I was funny. By Christmas, I had secured a girlfriend from the dance team—she gave me *lots* of attention. My parents were proud. I felt pretty good about myself.

But when high school was over, I headed to college. Comparing myself to the other basketball players who had been recruited, I didn't come close to their abilities (and ended up not even going out). My friends and parents were back home, a hundred miles away. My girlfriend was at a different college, two hundred miles away! No one was around to let me know how great I was. I had survived my teenage years on the "truths" they had told me, but when the voices couldn't be heard, their words had no real power to solve my loneliness. Though no one told me I was worthless, I felt like it. *Will I forever need the constant approval of others to feel good?* I thought.

I soon found out that until you know the truth of your worth to God, you'll always feel as if you don't quite measure up. Partial truths only stretch so far.

Why should you feel good about yourself? Have the words and attention from mere humans been enough to convince you your life has value?

God made a statement 2,000 years ago about your worth. "You're not a loser, but a winner. I created you, then when sin stole you away, I bought you back—ransomed by the Person most precious to Me: My Son, Jesus."

That type of truth should communicate more to you about your real worth in this world than any applause, kind words, awards, or female attention you might receive. If it doesn't, then your life will be half-filled with partial truths. Yes, you can survive being half-filled, but why would you want to?

Men who make an impact in life have learned to respond to the truth about their worth to God. They know they belong to God, so they know why they're here.

If you look at your answers from the "finish the sentence" at the beginning, you'll see that much of what you wrote has to do with things that you *do* or how you *look*. Hopefully, what you wrote about what God thinks of you is that He simply judges you for who you are. If not, you haven't heard the real truth of what the God of the Bible thinks of you. Let's review:

★ God made only one of you.

★ He made you for a reason.

★ There's nothing you can ever do to make Him love you less.

★ When others tell you lies or partial truths, compare them to the whole truth in the Bible.

ULTIMATE CHOICE

"Am I going to listen to the partial truths others say about me—and believe them? Or will I look to the truth of what God says and believe that?"

BOYS . . .

. . . believe only the half-truths people say to them.

MEN . . .

. . . give attention to the truth of God's Word about their worth. And then they realize how valuable they really are.

THE WORD

And I am convinced that nothing can ever separate us from his love. Death can't, and life can't.

Our fears for today, our worries about tomorrow, and even the powers of hell can't keep God's love away. Whether we are high above the sky or in the deepest ocean, nothing in all creation will ever be able to separate us from the love of God that is revealed in Christ Jesus our Lord.

ROMANS 8:38–39

For we are God's masterpiece. He has created us anew in Christ Jesus, so that we can do the good things he planned for us long ago.

EPHESIANS 2:10

When we were utterly helpless, Christ came at just the right time and died for us sinners. Now, no one is likely to die for a good person, though someone might be willing to die for a person who is especially good. But God showed his great love for us by sending Christ to die for us while we were still sinners.

ROMANS 5:6–8

ACTION IDEA

Talk to your mom and dad about how they viewed themselves when they were growing up. Ask them whom they listened to to realize how valuable they were.

9 *Humor without Hurting*

Plain and simple, when I was a young teenager I had a black belt in word warfare. I could cut a guy to pieces in front of a dozen people before he could get his tongue unraveled. Though I'd pick on anyone I thought was an easy target, there were two guys in particular who were easier than the rest.

Mark was overweight, said stupid things, and seemed to take my verbal barbs fairly well. I had been in Cub Scouts with him years before (and I actually liked him), but because he made it so easy to get a few laughs, I was always looking for ways to make him look like an idiot. The reason? So I'd look superior!

It worked.

Mike was a different story. He was the typical sixty-eight-pound weakling. He couldn't run faster than a slow walk. He threw a baseball like a girl. He couldn't even make a lay-in during intramurals—another easy target for my quick tongue that got me a lot of laughs.

When you're growing up you never think about the long-term effects your words have on another human being. You're trying to survive as best you can. You want to be noticed and popular. And usually, you don't care who lies on the mat after you deliver your verbal knockout punch as the crowd declares you champion.

By the time these two guys reached their senior year in high school, both were so socially inept you could almost predict they'd be voted most likely to go fade into oblivion, never to be heard from again. All because of guys like me.

In college I became a Christian. One day I came upon this verse: "With his mouth the godless destroys his neighbor, but through knowledge the righteous escape" (Proverbs 11:9, NIV).

"The godless destroys his neighbor." I didn't have God in my life, and I certainly knew that I'd contributed to at least partially destroying another soul whom God had created.

How about you? Are you good at making your friends laugh at someone else's expense? Or, has someone else's jokes and cutting remarks directed at you ever hurt your feelings?

It's been proven that most of us speak 25,000 to 30,000 words a day. That means we're no doubt going to fail! We're going to let a word slip we shouldn't, or a remark about someone that hurts them but makes us look momentarily cool.

The main issue to God, however, isn't just our words—it's our heart. Jesus said, "A good person produces good deeds from a good heart, and an evil person produces evil deeds from an evil heart. Whatever is in your heart determines what you say" (Luke 6:45). I had a heart problem, and I showed the world how messed up it was by what I said. The apostle Paul identified my problem to perfection: "When I was a child, I spoke and thought and reasoned as a child does. But when I grew up, I put away childish things" (1 Corinthians 13:11).

Humor is great. There's nothing wrong with having a quick wit. But when it's used to destroy your neighbor, it shows you're still a boy with at least a partially evil heart. To change, you don't need a lecture or a finger wagging in your face. But you do need to recognize this immaturity in your heart and have the desire to grow up.

The mouth, however, is something you can't fix on your own. "No one can tame the tongue. It is an uncontrollable evil, full of deadly poison. Sometimes it praises our Lord and Father, and sometimes it breaks out into curses against those who have been made in the image of God" (James 3:8–9).

For a boy to grow up in how he uses his mouth, he needs two things:

1. A best friend. Without at least one other person (perhaps more) to help remind you to keep the put-downs to a minimum—who has permission to slug you when you go overboard—you'll likely fall into the same habits of word warfare.

2. The Holy Spirit—every day. If you're not intentionally asking God's Spirit to tame your tongue several times each day, you'll be trying to fix it on your own. And the passage from James says "no one can tame the tongue." But God can! . . . if you'll ask Him.

I read a quote a while back that has always stuck with me. "Cold words freeze people, and hot words scorch them, and bitter words make them bitter, and wrathful words make them wrathful. Kind words also produce their own image on men's souls; and a beautiful image it is. They soothe, quiet and comfort the hearer" (Blaise Pascal).

I wasn't the only guy who was using Mark and Mike as verbal punching bags, but I know that I perhaps could have produced a different image on their soul—a beautiful image. Take a minute to examine yourself and the image you're putting on the soul of others around you. And if you need to, start allowing your "humor" process toward manhood to move a little quicker.

ULTIMATE CHOICE

"Will I be careless with the way I use my mouth, using it to hurt people if it feels good or gives me attention, or will I learn how to hold my tongue?"

BOYS . . .

. . . say whatever it takes to get noticed, no matter whom it hurts.

MEN . . .

. . . realize that words are like weapons; that it's important to choose what they say wisely because they can hurt the soul of another whom God has created in His image.

It is foolish to belittle a neighbor; a person with good sense remains silent.

PROVERBS 11:12

The godly person gives wise advice, but the tongue that deceives will be cut off. The godly speak words that are helpful, but the wicked speak only what is corrupt.

PROVERBS 10:31–32

ACTION IDEA

Think of one person whom you've hurt with your words and apologize to him or her for what has been said.

10

What You Set Your Eyes On

The fog was the pea soup variety. Thick and not too tasty. But an F-15 pilot was trained to put his wheels down in any kind of weather. As the eleven-year fighter pilot veteran kept his eyes focused on his instruments, he knew what would bring him in safely: listening to the tower.

Making his approach from three miles out, his radio crackled.

"Ramrod, you're coming in a little steep," the tower radioman calmly reported. "Push down another six degrees. And Ramrod, our instruments tell us you're coming in upside down. Better do a one-eighty."

"Did you say upside down, tower?"

"That's a roger, Ramrod."

Looking up and around gave the pilot no new info on his attitude. And the amber lights reflecting against the Plexiglas ceiling couldn't help gain his orientation. However, he *knew* he was flying right-side-up.

Two miles from touchdown.

"Ramrod, you're looking good. Bank two degrees left, put your wheels down, and keep your decline steady," came the voice from his headset. "And you still need to make that one-eighty."

"Tower, would you check your instruments? I have no confidence I'm needing to right this bird."

"Roger, Ramrod. Checking."

One mile.

Waiting in the dark brings a lonely fear a pilot gets used to, but this type of waiting gets the sweat beads popping.

"That's affirm, Ramrod. This is a no-doubter. You need to do that one-eighty immediately, cut your airspeed, and give me one-half degree left. I repeat: one-eighty immediately."

Fighting against his senses that scream against the tower's instructions, but knowing the confidence he must have in that unseen voice in the darkness, Ramrod pleads one more time.

"Tower, I'm feeling like I'm coming in straight up."

"Ramrod, you must do that one-eighty . . . NOW!"

With a twist of his stick, Ramrod obeys.

Within two seconds, he feels the sudden bump as his back wheels hit pavement.

Obeying that unseen voice went against everything that veteran pilot knew—and thought—to be true. Yet it was life and death. The fact remains, he had a choice: follow the instructions of the man whose job it was to bring him in safely, or trust his own senses.

Since you're growing into manhood, you're likely making more and more of your own choices. As it relates to what you set your eyes on, you've probably been somewhat guarded by your parents for many years. They know that it's not healthy to simply allow you to watch whatever you want, so they've made choices for you.

If you haven't gained media freedom already, you'll obtain it when you leave home. You'll be free to feast on anything the tube, the screen, or magazines want you to gaze at. You'll find that it's different, often more exciting, enticing, and arousing than what your parents have let you see. Since many of your friends will talk about what they've seen, you'll have a curiosity about what you're missing.

But there's a radioman inside of your head, isn't there? He's saying what your parents have hopefully said: "Not everything you put into your brain is good, Son. Be careful not to allow any junk inside, because it will be hard to get out."

Many of the images, however, will *seem* OK. The voice of the crowd has a way of disorienting you. Your own feelings seem to shout, "What's so wrong with it?"

Much of the media is like that pea soup fog the pilot faced. It clouds reality, and it's impossible to get rid of. Yet if it's allowed to disorient you into making decisions about what goes through your eyes and into your brain, it's as deadly as hard pavement at two hundred miles per hour. Not the immediate type of deadly, but the slow kind—the kind that's tough to notice, but stronger than any slow poison ever made.

What makes it even more complicated is it's not the body the media destroys, it's the soul. And the soul of a man needs purity if he is going to land safely.

The mind makes the choice. The eyes allow the junk. The memory has another image imprinted. Multiply these images many times, and what you see is what you become. No, not overnight. Not even within a few years. But over time (as is Satan's patient strategy), the soul has crash-landed.

The results become evident: a toleration to profanity (even using the Lord's name in vain), blurred lines between good and evil, and for many men, an addiction to pornography. It never happens all at once, but it *always* begins through what the mind allows the eyes to look at.

ULTIMATE CHOICE

"Will I allow my mind to be polluted with anything just because it's on TV or the big screen, or will I recognize garbage, and choose not to let it in?"

BOYS . . .

. . . let their eyes take in anything in front of them, not realizing the impact repeated viewings is having on them.

MEN . . .

. . . set no worthless thing before their eyes. They value their mind and future too much to not be discerning and selective. They have the courage and self-control to use their choices to protect their future today.

_____**THE WORD**_____

I will refuse to look at anything vile and vulgar.
PSALM 101:3A

*And now, dear friends, let me say one more
thing as I close this letter. Fix your thoughts on what
is true and honorable and right. Think about things
that are pure and lovely and admirable. Think
about things that are excellent and worthy of praise.*
PHILIPPIANS 4:8

ACTION IDEA

Talk through what the viewing guidelines are with your
parents. Hear their arguments and, if necessary, challenge
what *their* habits have been. Decide on some guidelines you
both can agree on.

Learn to ask yourself the tough questions: *Is this show,
this movie, this magazine, this music really talking about
values I want to have? Am I being subtly influenced in a
direction I don't want to go?*

11   *You're Gifted!*

Ever wonder where you fit in a world filled with nearly six *billion* people?

Did you ever say to yourself, *Self, why are you taking up space? Why did God bother to create you? What are you going to do with your life? Will you be special or just another ordinary Joe who goes through life never making any difference?*

Sooner or later, you're going to realize that to 99.999 percent of the world you'll always be a "last name, first name, social security number." If you haven't already had these questioning thoughts, you likely will by the time you register for your first term in college—especially if it's a big college.

When these questions pop into your head, you'll go on a search—a search for significance. Some adults hit that trail and seem to never get off of it. Their whole life is spent trying to "find themselves" and to answer a few of the questions asked above.

Great news! Your search is over . . . if you want it to be.

The reason: God has placed you on earth for a purpose. He's created you, and if you let Him, He'll show you why He made you—every day. He's not only gifted you, but he's *gifting* you, even as you read these pages. I'm not referring to the "spiritual gifts" in 1 Corinthians 12, but the motivational-type gifts and talents that God gives to everyone.

Here are a few of the facts:

★ "God has given each of us the ability to do certain things well" (Romans 12:6).

40

Do you see the words "except you" in that passage? No, and you won't, because it *includes* you!

What kind of gift is it? Why was it given?

✭ "However, he has given each one of us a special gift according to the generosity of Christ. That is why the Scriptures say, 'When he ascended to the heights, he led a crowd of captives and gave gifts to his people'" (Ephesians 4:7–8).

You have a special gift because of the *generosity of Christ.* Why have you been given special gifts?

✭ "God has given gifts to each of you from his great variety of spiritual gifts. Manage them well so that God's generosity can flow through you" (1 Peter 4:10). Another translation is even more to the point. "Each one should use whatever gift he has received to serve others, faithfully administering God's grace in its various forms" (NIV).

You are given gifts to serve—to be used by God to show His grace to others.

Time out for a quick matching quiz. Take a pencil and match the famous personality with his talent.

Person	Talent
1. Barry Bonds	a. Singer
2. Jay Leno	b. Basketball
3. Michael W. Smith	c. Comedy
4. Shaquille O'Neal	d. Preaching
5. Billy Graham	e. Baseball

OK, so that was pretty easy. The obvious point is that some people who are given gifts and talents most of the world would die for, don't use them to serve God, but to serve themselves. Athletes, musicians, communicators—you and me—we all have a choice to use what we've been given for *our* glory or *God's* glory. But there's another choice we have that is illustrated in a passage from Luke 19:12–26. Let me give you the short, slightly updated version.

A company president had to go out of town for some important business, but before he left, he gave ten associates some cash to invest while he was gone. When the president returned he asked the ten what his investment had made. One guy made ten times the original amount! Needless to say, his boss was happy, so he put him in charge of ten small companies. Another guy made five times what he was originally given, so he was given five companies. But one guy, thinking he should do the safe thing, just put the money in his mattress. His boss wasn't happy at all! "You could have at least put the money in the bank," he told the guy, "then I'd have made a little interest on it." Returning to the original story, here's what happened:

"Then turning to the others standing nearby, the king ordered, 'Take the money from this servant, and give it to the one who earned the most.'

"'But, master,' they said, 'that servant has enough already!'

"'Yes,' the king replied, 'but to those who use well what they are given, even more will be given. But from those who are unfaithful, even what little they have will be taken away'" (vv. 24–26).

Did you catch the point? "Use it or lose it." It also says that if you use your gifts correctly, you could get more.

In order to know why God created them, men

* ⋆ know they are gifted by God;
* ⋆ do what they can to learn what their gifts and talents are;
* ⋆ use them to glorify God and point others to His grace;
* ⋆ are often rewarded by having their gifts and talents multiplied beyond their wildest expectations.

Think about all of the people you know who have used their gifts to help make your life better in some way (school teachers, coaches, pastors, parents, friends). God has used—and continues to use—all of these people to help make you into a man of God. Without them you would have been less than you could have been.

Now it's your turn to do the same in the lives of those around you. Once you start using your gifts and talents to *give* instead of *take,* you'll never again doubt why God has placed you here on earth. You'll understand why the real fun of being a Christian is being used by God to help others.

ULTIMATE CHOICE

"Will I realize that I'm uniquely gifted by God to help others, or will I use my talents and abilities to make my own life better?"

BOYS . . .

. . . either don't bother recognizing what their gifts are, or use their talents to only draw attention to themselves.

MEN . . .

. . . seek after God to discover their gifts, then use them to help others.

THE WORD

He is the one who gave these gifts to the church: the apostles, the prophets, the evangelists, and the pastors and teachers. Their responsibility is to equip God's people to do his work and build up the church, the body of Christ, until we come to such unity in our faith and knowledge of God's Son that we will be mature and full grown in the Lord, measuring up to the full stature of Christ.

EPHESIANS 4:11–13

ACTION IDEA

Think about one of the many things you do well. How can you use that talent to help someone this week?

12   *Who's Afraid of the Big, Bad...?*

uick multiple choice: When you were younger, what were you most afraid of?

 a. the dark

 b. having bad dreams

 c. your dad

 d. monsters

 e. closed-in places

 f. being left alone

 g. the water

 h. the school bully

 i. scary movies

 j. heights

 k. going to school

 l. other:_____

True confessions time. For me (in my *very* younger years, of course), it was snakes under the bed . . . monsters in the closet . . . and mosquitos in the dark. By the time I hit junior high, I had conquered the first two (without a night-light, I might add), and learned how to squish the mosquitos on the wall before they had the chance to take dive bombing practice on my ears. But my teenage years didn't rid my life of fear. I'd taken on a few others to replace them:

* ✯ talking to girls
* ✯ my parents getting a divorce
* ✯ what those in my grade thought of me

By high school I'd almost conquered talking to girls, my parents had each been through two divorces (so I was used to the routine), but I still couldn't kill that fear-of-the-crowd mosquito. It was always buzzing around my head ready to bite my ear. What was I trying to use to swat that insecurity with?

* ✯ By occasionally partying, I gained the approval of the drinking and dope-smoking crowd. (Swat.)
* ✯ By playing sports, I got the approval from all of the friends and strangers who thought athletics was a ticket to popularity. (Swat, swat.)

I kept swatting at this insecurity, but never did squish it.

By looking at my own progression, it's easy to notice that some fears you grow out of, others you learn to deal with, and a few stick with you, always buzzing around your head. For most guys, the fear of the crowd is the constant buzz. I probably couldn't have admitted how much my friends controlled what I did. My actions, however, told the real story. They affected almost every area of my life:

* ✯ how I dressed
* ✯ what music I listened to
* ✯ how I talked
* ✯ how much I studied (and what grades I got)
* ✯ what I did on weekends

I didn't know how to be myself so I settled for being who I *thought* people wanted me to be. My fear of not being accepted by the crowd actually made me become someone God didn't intend for me to be. Once I began to follow the Lord closely in college, I learned to be comfortable with me! I didn't need to go along to get along. Yes, I lost a few "friends," but God replaced them with people who truly had *my* best interest at heart. It wasn't easy losing those friends, but it was worth it.

How can you conquer this fear?

Look at your own life. It's not a sin to act like your friends or to do the things they want you to do, but it's foolishness to let your fear of losing a friend's approval take you down a road opposite of what you know to be the right one.

Does your list match mine from a couple paragraphs above? If so, it's time to put God to the test. Ask Him to help you set the pace instead of blindly following the pace set by others. Above all, learn what David learned: *"The fear of the LORD is the beginning of wisdom"* (Psalm 111:10, NIV). This type of fear reveres Him above anything else; ii does not mean you are frightened of God. It realizes that "if God is for me, who can be against me?"

ULTIMATE CHOICE

"Will I allow my fears—especially fear of the crowd—to prevent me from becoming the man God wants me to be, or will I go boldly where few men ever go—beyond their fears?"

BOYS . . .

. . . live in fear of the crowd, thinking that if they don't act like everyone else, they won't have any friends.

MEN . . .

. . . want God's approval above all else; they realize that fearing Him allows them to be released from the fear of what others think.

THE WORD

The LORD is for me, so I will not be afraid. What can mere mortals do to me? Yes, the LORD is for me; he will help me. I will look in triumph at those who hate me. It is better to trust the LORD *than to put confidence in people. It is better to trust the* LORD *than to put confidence in princes.*

PSALM 118:6–9

The LORD *is my light and my salvation—so why should I be afraid? The* LORD *protects me from danger—so why should I tremble? When evil people come to destroy me, when my enemies and foes attack me, they will stumble and fall. Though a mighty army surrounds me, my heart will know no fear. Even if they attack me, I remain confident.*

PSALM 27:1–3

ACTION IDEA

Be honest and think: What do you do or not do, say or not say, around your friends that you wouldn't do, not do, say, or not say around your parents (or God)? If the list is more than a few items, your fear of the crowd is great. It's time to learn the freedom that comes when only God is feared and revered.

13   Learning to Be a Promise Keeper

"I'll do my homework right after the game. I promise."

"I made a promise to God to stay a virgin until I get married. I even filled out a card and signed my name to it."

"The guys want me to go out for bowling and pizza tonight. I'll do my chores tomorrow. I promise."

"Dad, if you let me go out for baseball, I'll stick with it all year no matter whether I play or ride the bench. I promise."

"I promised my grandpa I wouldn't drink or take drugs all through high school. He said he'd give me $500 at graduation if I stayed clean."

Guys are good at tossing out promises, but they don't always make a completion every throw. Just ask Pete Newell.

Pete went to camp one summer and came back extremely stoked for the Lord. He was challenged to value what God values, so on the van ride back he made a list of five promises he'd keep no matter what:

1. He'd never cheat on tests.

2. He wouldn't touch a girl any place that was covered by clothes.

3. He wouldn't break the curfew his parents gave him.

4. He'd start a lunchtime Bible study at his school.

5. He wouldn't swear on the court during basketball season.

When January rolled around, Pete had broken three of them! Naturally, he felt bad. But not about breaking his promises. He was ticked at the speaker for even suggesting he make them.

"They should have told me I couldn't keep them all," he said. He vowed never to make another big promise again. Dealing with the failure and guilt wasn't worth the hassle.

What do you think is Pete's problem?

★ Is he a weakling without a backbone?

★ Was he too hasty in making those promises?

★ Is he not a very strong Christian?

★ Does he just not understand how God's grace can help him stand firm?

★ Can any teen guy keep all the promises he makes to himself or God?

No. Maybe. Perhaps. Yes. No.

Pete's dilemma isn't a matter of making promises that are too big or setting goals that are too high. He's simply not being patient with himself: a sixteen-year-old who is still under construction.

It's obvious Pete isn't a boy. It's equally clear he's not quite a man. Yet he chose to make "man-size" promises. That alone means he's closer to being a man than most. But by choosing to quit making promises, Pete is saying he's still got a little bit of boy in him, too.

As you know, a lot goes into the making of a man. More than what could fit into one chapter (or one book). But here are five things real men understand:

Real men want control. No, not the "control over girls, people, money, and cars" you hear about from the media. Real men want control over themselves. They know that boys say yes to their urges, while men know the *what, when,* and *how* to say no. To his credit, Pete knew the *what* and *when,* but he hadn't learned the *how* part takes time.

Real men have convictions. Knowing right from wrong doesn't make someone a man of conviction. Those values have to be exercised and tested before they really work. Pete should have realized that his commitment to do right and not compromise would be tested. Anything worth valuing—especially if it's one of God's values—will get Satan's attention. The deceiver wants to convince you that acting on God's standards is too tough, too demanding, and too stupid if you want to have a social life.

Pete was on the right track, but his timeline for success was just too short. He felt that if he couldn't keep his promises the first time out, he might just as well give up.

Real men take responsibility. Instead of blaming their failures on someone else, real men admit that their actions don't always match their convictions. Pete blamed the speaker for planting in him the idea of making promises. He couldn't bring himself to admit that he'd made poor choices. He thought that by saying, "I blew it," he would somehow be less of a man. Actually, just the opposite is true.

Real men understand God's grace. Though Pete's brain knew God was always forgiving, his heart hadn't grasped how much God was on his team. The key is understanding that our heavenly Father is unfailingly persistent. This is the most powerful weapon available to a boy who wants to become a man.

God isn't shaking His finger at us when a promise is broken. Instead, He's picking us up, dusting us off, and encouraging us to keep trying. All the while He's pointing us onward and upward. That's how grace works for the believer—it motivates us to keep moving. Not understanding His grace grinds us to a halt.

Real men know they can't make it alone. Totally left out of Pete's strategy were other guys walking with him, helping him keep his promises. Boys who believe they need to go through life flying solo are destined to remain boys. Real manhood can't be achieved alone. Without lots of prayer, encouragement, and an occasional kick in the pants from other males, you will fall—again and again. If you don't have other guys you can talk to about anything, forget real manhood.

ULTIMATE CHOICE

"When challenged to make significant promises, will I back off from making them so I won't fail, or will I allow God's grace to move me forward so that I can be the promise keeper I want to be?"

BOYS . . .

. . . get frustrated with their failures and give up, never seeing the fruit of sticking with something for the long haul.

MEN . . .

. . . realize they're going to sometimes break a promise, but because they have set high standards for themselves, they continue to press on—with God's grace—to be the man they want to be.

THE WORD

Don't let anyone think less of you because you are young. Be an example to all believers in what you teach, in the way you live, in your love, your faith, and your purity.

1 TIMOTHY 4:12

Therefore, since we are surrounded by such a huge crowd of witnesses to the life of faith, let us strip off every weight that slows us down, especially the sin that so easily hinders our progress. And let us run with endurance the race that God has set before us.

HEBREWS 12:1

ACTION IDEA

If you want to learn more about what makes a real man—and you'd also like to spend a couple of days with dad or grandpa—then maybe you should plan a trip to an upcoming "Promise Keeper" conference. They're designed specifically to challenge men to true Christian manhood. Most churches are aware of the upcoming "Promise Keeper" events. Call your church office to find out, or for more information about this movement, call (303) 421-2800 or write Promise Keepers, P.O. Box 18376, Boulder, CO 80308.

14 Deserving of Honor

There's a passage of Scripture you've likely heard before—many times before, perhaps too many times before: "'Honor your father and mother.' This is the first of the Ten Commandments that ends with a promise. And this is the promise: If you honor your father and mother, 'you will live a long life, full of blessing'" (Ephesians 6:2–3).

Here's how Webster defines *honor*: "high regard or great respect given, received, or enjoyed. Something done or given as a token or act of respect."

If you're serious about moving from boyhood to Christian manhood, you can't ignore this command. It's one of the few passages in the Bible that is specifically addressed to you. And did you notice? It doesn't give an age when you are to start or finish.

Honoring your father and mother is a lifetime job! And this key point you shouldn't miss: Honoring your parents doesn't begin when you're safely out of your bratty, early adolescent years. The Bible doesn't account for hormones and puberty and growth spurts that make you moody. But it *does* give a promise to you if honor is given, "you will live a long life, full of blessing." Another version says, "that it may go well with you and that you may enjoy long life on the earth" (NIV).

What does honor look like? Is it blindly passive whenever an order is barked from a parent's mouth? Do you stay quiet when things aren't fair? Do you sit in your room all the time so you don't cause any trouble?

No, no, and no.

At this point in your life, you and your parents are in a battle for independence. You're doing what comes naturally—breaking away from your parents so you'll be ready to go it alone when it's time to leave the nest. Your parents are also doing what comes naturally—holding onto you for dear life because they "can't believe their baby is growing up so fast and he'll soon be leaving home." In case you didn't know, this is the reason why there's occasional conflict in the home. It has nothing to do with curfew, cars, not going to church, or wanting to spend more time with the guys. You're both simply doing what comes naturally.

Most parents are perceptive enough to know they need to cut their son some slack. But only a few kids are perceptive enough to realize how hard it is for their parents to let go. Those that know what's going on have a fairly easy time of it their last few years at home. Those that don't, don't. And that's when honor gets left in the dust.

Again, what does honor look like?

The heart of honoring your parents is realizing that God has placed them in your life to help prepare you for adulthood (that place where you'll spend most of your years). It's a tough job, and one where they'll make mistakes. Honoring your parents, however, means realizing that God is even using their mistakes to mold your life and character. It doesn't seem like it, but you actually grow more into a man not by what you do when you know they're right, but what you do when you think (or know) they're wrong. What's the promise if you *do* show honor? "A long life, full of blessing."

Honor means not talking back disrespectfully in "that tone" or with "that attitude." The promise: "a long life, full of blessing."

When a command is made that seems unfair, giving honor means that after calmly discussing it with your parents, logically presenting your side, you end up obeying the final decision. The promise: "a long life, full of blessing."

When jobs aren't apportioned correctly, or you're being disciplined for something you didn't do, honor means looking your parents in the eye and letting them know by your voice inflection, body language, and sincerity of your words that they're being unfair or making a mistake. If you've built up a bank account of trust because of your honesty, your point will be made and fairness will be restored. But if not, honor means carrying through with the final parental conclusion. The promise: "a long life, full of blessing." (Please note: Promises aren't always fulfilled the exact moment you want them. But hang with it. Don't settle for getting your way in the short-term. If you exemplify honor, you'll win their trust in the long-term, which is really what you want.)

Do you get the picture?

Honor is a gift that holds the honoree in high regard. Sometimes beyond what *you think* they deserve. It should be mentioned that some homes have unbelieving parents. God can even use them! A few homes have stepparents or parents who are doing things to their child that are clearly wrong. Each situation is different, and in these situations, much of what this chapter is talking about may not apply.

God wants it to go well with you and to make sure you have a "long life on earth." Prisons and drug rehab hospitals are filled with people who wanted to get out from their parents' authority. They chose not to honor and respect them, did their own thing, now they are faced with a long life, but not a happy one.

Honor is the daily decision *men* make, not to get their own way, but because it's the right thing to do.

ULTIMATE CHOICE

"Will I choose to show my parents the honor and respect they deserve, or will I show by my actions and words that I want to live my own life apart from their influence?"

BOYS . . .

. . . fail to see how important it is to show their parents honor.

MEN . . .

. . . honor their parents by their actions and their words—
and God honors them because of it.

THE WORD

*A wise child brings joy to a father; a foolish
child brings grief to a mother.*

PROVERBS 10:1

*Whoever stubbornly refuses to accept criticism
will suddenly be broken beyond repair.*

PROVERBS 29:1

ACTION IDEA

This week, think of one or more ways you can honor
your parents—and do it.

15

It's All About Relationships

If you haven't learned it already, you soon will: Sometimes, being a Christian can sure be weird.

The beliefs and lifestyle God wants you to take as your own go against your ego, your hormones, and what most other people are doing. To follow God closely as a Christian man means obeying these "weird" and "unnatural" commands as if they were personally delivered to you by Jesus Christ Himself. One that I've always thought was a bit over the edge *was* delivered by Jesus. Get this: "So if you are standing before the altar in the Temple, offering a sacrifice to God, and you suddenly remember that someone has something against you, leave your sacrifice there beside the altar. Go and be reconciled to that person. Then come and offer your sacrifice to God" (Matthew 5:23–24).

You and I don't offer gifts at altars, do we? But we do pray, we do worship, we do try to win God's favor so our life will be smoother. What God is saying is that *before* you do any of these, think about all of the people you know. Do any of these people have a problem with you? Have you intentionally done something that has offended them? Have you done something *unintentionally* that perhaps offended them?

That's exactly what this passage is asking.

The question is: Why would God want me to do something this radical? Why must I go above and beyond what the rest of the world is even thinking about?

The reason: Relationships are *everything* to God! Right behavior is important. A knowledge of Scripture is essential. But right relationships are where God lives—and dies.

Jesus Christ didn't suffer and die on the cross because we didn't know the Bible backwards and forwards. He didn't willingly take our sin because we couldn't get our act together and be perfect like Him. No, He lived, taught, suffered, died, and rose again because God wanted us to truly know Him—to see the depth of His love for us.

It has always been about relationships!

From the garden of Eden until today, it's been the main thing to God. Two types of relationships are intertwined together: (1) our relationship with Him and (2) our relationship with our fellow man. If we have bad relationships with people whom we can see every day, we cannot be so bold as to say we have a good relationship with an invisible God whom we've never laid eyes on.

That's why Jesus can make this challenge. It's logical. It fits with what is true. And He exemplified it to the uttermost. He took the initiative to make us right with God—even when we didn't know something was wrong. He left His kingly realm after we shook our fist at God and told Him we'd rather do it our own way. It was His initiative taken on account of our sin that made a good relationship with God possible for you and me.

If you want to be a Christian man who has a right relationship with God, you must see that this weird challenge in Matthew makes perfect sense. You must obey it.

If you've hurt a female by what you've said or done, go to her and tell her you're sorry. (If you're not sure, go and find out.)

If you've shown disrespect to another adult or parent, look that person in the eye and tell him or her you were wrong. (If you're not sure, go and find out.)

If you've offended another guy—friend or not—make a phone call and apologize. (If you're not sure, find out.)

When you do this, you'll be showing the world what God wants them to know: relationships are the main thing. By your humble efforts, others may be drawn to the Father. Plus, you'll feel a freedom and a peace you've never known. You're not responsible for whether they accept your apology; you're only responsible for being obedient enough to make things right. Effort and intent is what God most wants to see.

ULTIMATE CHOICE

"Will I choose to take the initiative in my relationships, asking for forgiveness from those I've wronged, or will I believe it doesn't matter and pretend the problem doesn't exist?"

BOYS . . .

. . . ask forgiveness only when there isn't another way out of the situation.

MEN . . .

. . . know that having clean relationships with everyone allows them to come to God with a clear conscience and could very well point the way for others to come to Him as well.

THE WORD

Do your part to live in peace with everyone, as much as possible.

ROMANS 12:18

If someone says, "I love God," but hates another Christian, that person is a liar; for if we don't love people we can see, how can we love God, whom we have not seen?

1 JOHN 4:20

ACTION IDEA

Go through a mental checklist of those you know. Make a list of those who may have something against you. In the next month, make contact with them and try to get it cleared up, asking for forgiveness when appropriate.

16

Tearing Down the Walls of Sin

ultiple choice quiz time again. To what would you compare your conscience?

- a. a rooster crowing
- b. a tea kettle that slowly boils to a whistle
- c. a smoke alarm
- d. a dead goldfish easily flushed
- e. a distant police siren that gets louder the closer it gets
- f. an intercom system so filled with static, you can't understand all that's being said
- g. a quiet voice from a best friend you've grown to trust

During your preschool years, your parents were the ones who corrected you as you were getting yourself in trouble. A spank, a look, and a firm voice all served to make sure you didn't touch something hot, drink something poisonous, or run out in front of a car. You're still alive, so all of their efforts succeeded.

In grade school it was fifty-thirty-twenty. Fifty percent of the time your parents used the same tactics, thirty percent your teachers kept you in line, and twenty percent you were on your own. (That twenty percent is why you still were punished during those years!)

★ In junior high the percentages change: thirty-thirty-forty.

★ In high school they change again: twenty-twenty-sixty.

★ By the time you graduate and hit college, it's five-five-ninety.

That type of freedom is wonderful, but it comes with a price tag. If you don't listen to the right voices, *you* pay the consequences. It's *your* property that gets damaged; *your* health that gets ruined; *your* relationships that are broken; *your* spiritual life that suffers.

From your earliest years, God has been using people in your life to build a conscience—your internal voice that lets you know when you're getting too close to a cliff. Some guys, in their desire to throw off the "controls" by those who care about them, choose to build a wall around that conscience. When they get closer to the cliff, they don't want to hear any voices, roosters, alarm clocks—or even the voice of a trusted friend. They want to do what *they* want to do.

Steve was raised in a strong Christian home, went to church camps, and was even baptized. But when he was old enough, he started going to R-rated movies (without his parents' knowledge). In college, his language, attitude, and the things he wanted to do for fun began to match what he heard on the screen. It brought him new friends—non-Christian friends. Within two years he had chosen to forget about going to church, forget about reading his Bible and praying, forget about everything he'd been taught as a child. He flushed that fish that had once been a good relationship with God. He was soon renting X-rated videos and going to bars. Within four years he had slept with so many girls he'd lost count. And, sadly, within four years he had contracted a sexually transmitted disease that will eventually kill him through a slow and agonizing death (yes, AIDS).

As you grow out of boyhood into manhood, sin becomes more enticing. And when you allow even one sin to go unconfessed to God, it leaves a brick between you and your conscience—between you and God. Many sins means many bricks.

What do you do when you have so many bricks you think you can never tear them down? Steve found out. He hit bottom before he began to humble himself and confess those sins that were once a strong wall. It didn't take long for him to realize that when the bricks were gone, he could see God again for who He is: a trusted friend.

Large or small, you won't be able to keep from occasionally adding bricks—and a wall—between you and God. Perhaps there is one there now. Maybe you've fooled everyone else, but even you know you can't fool yourself. There's a distance between you and God and that wall of sin is the reason.

What are you going to do about it?

Let me encourage you: There is a trusted friend on the other side of that wall. He's ready and willing to forgive; He's just waiting for you to ask. How do I know? His Word says so.

As you consider whether to get rid of those bricks, consider what God has to say in His Word.

Who has sinned? "For all have sinned; all fall short of God's glorious standard" (Romans 3:23). Sin is missing God's standard for entrance into His presence on earth and in heaven: sinlessness. It's a disease all humans have.

What are the consequences? "But there is a problem— your sins have cut you off from God. Because of your sin, he has turned away and will not listen anymore" (Isaiah 59:2). When those sin bricks are between you and God, it's tough for Him to hear you. They must first be removed.

"For the wages of sin is death, but the free gift of God is eternal life through Christ Jesus our Lord" (Romans 6:23). If those bricks stay strong between God and you throughout your life, they separate you from His presence—forever. It truly will be a living eternal hell.

How do we get rid of sin? "Have mercy on me, O God, because of your unfailing love. Because of your great compassion, blot out the stain of my sins. Wash me clean from my guilt. Purify me from my sin. For I recognize my shameful deeds—they haunt me day and night" (Psalm 51:1–3). This prayer, said from the humble heart of a sinner (David), is the type God *always* answers!

"But if we confess our sins to him, he is faithful and just to forgive us and to cleanse us from every wrong" (1 John 1:9). There is no mention here of "extra bad" sins that can't be forgiven. Whatever you've done—or will do—He is faithful to forgive and cleanse. Confession is turning around and heading God's direction. It's been said that no matter how far you walk away from God, when you turn around He's right next to you.

Do we have to do more than repent? "Prove by the way you live that you have really turned from your sins and turned to God" (Matthew 3:8). Repentance without change only starts rebuilding that wall of sin between you and God. He doesn't expect instant perfection, but He does want you to progress in your obedience to His Word and the conscience He uses to speak to you.

Does God remember our sin once we've confessed it? "I— yes, I alone—am the one who blots out your sins for my own sake and will never think of them again" (Isaiah 43:25). When God says He forgets something, He forgets it! He doesn't want you carrying around a load of guilt. And He certainly doesn't want you imagining there's a wall between you two when He died to assure you that wall had been torn down for good!

The key to keeping that wall torn down between you and God is believing your conscience is a trusted friend who only wants the best for your life.

ULTIMATE CHOICE

"Will I ignore my conscience and disregard small sins, or will I learn how refreshing it is to ask for forgiveness and get clean with God?"

BOYS . . .

. . . don't understand sin's magnitude—even small sins— and come to God only when they're sorry they got caught.

MEN . . .

. . . are quick to come to God to confess sin, and realize that though God doesn't take sin lightly, He is faithful to always forgive.

THE WORD

Now turn from your sins and turn to God, so you can be cleansed of your sins. Then wonderful times of refreshment will come from the presence of the Lord, and he will send Jesus your Messiah to you again.

ACTS 3:19–20

ACTION IDEA

Since God is ready, willing, and able to tear that wall of sin down, you should be, too. Take some time and confess your sin to God—brick by brick—so that times of refreshing may come from His presence!

17   *Real Friends*

Up until my late junior year in high school, I was a pretty good kid. I'd lived alone with my mother for a few years, and, well, her life as a struggling, lonely, single mom was tough enough already. She didn't need a son going off the deep end to complicate a life already in major disarray. Fortunately, the friends I'd chosen were good ones. In an era when a high percentage of students were taking drugs and partying all the time, my group didn't.

But in the spring of my junior year, all of that changed. A few of my "fringe friends" started talking to me about smoking dope. They were a bit more popular than my normal friends, so I listened. Then I tried it. By summer, when I was working full-time and making good money in a bean cannery, I was getting high *every day*.

What did my old friends do? Nothing. Since I had abandoned them, they didn't come after me to tell me I was heading down the wrong road. Maybe they thought I wouldn't listen. Perhaps they were right. But I wish they would have thought enough of our friendship to at least once have talked to me about it.

At the time, I thought it was all pretty harmless. But I remember that on a number of mind-altered occasions I *should not* have been driving—or riding with those who were. Too young. Too dumb. Too intent on getting into a more popular group. God was protecting me, I later discovered, and I'm incredibly thankful He was.

Whether you're in a public or private school, the chances are high that one of your friends will begin to leisurely stroll down the wrong path. At the start of that road to destruction, they won't seem so far away from you. Perhaps you won't even notice they've veered off the straight and narrow. But when you *do* see there's some distance between you that wasn't there before, what are you going to do?

Say, "It's their life. I'm not perfect. I'm not God. They know right from wrong."

Those four sentences in that brief quote are all true. And sometimes people are going to head off the deep end no matter who challenges them. But a true friend warns another that if they're swimming with sharks, it's time to get out of the water.

Perhaps you'll think, *Hey, if I decide to head a different direction, I certainly wouldn't want someone in my face telling me what to do.*

Fair enough. Don't *tell* them what to do. Instead . . .

* ★ Express your concern.

* ★ Fight the urge to make it a selfish plea to have things be like they used to.

* ★ Admit to them that you make your own share of mistakes. Ask them if you've done anything to set them off.

* ★ Show them specifically what you've noticed and ask them if you're coming to the right conclusions.

* ★ Let them talk. Perhaps there are reasons why they've headed away from the right path (like a disintegrating family situation).

* ★ If you think it's needed, bring another friend or two with you to show your concern and support as a group. (Fight the urge to tell them they're being a jerk. That will only confirm to them they were right about changing groups.)

★ Ask them if you could go with them to have a talk with your youth leader or Sunday school teacher. Sometimes having an adult ear and some extra wisdom is needed.

★ Point them back to the faith they once professed, without making them feel like God's going to abandon them if they don't. Remind them how loving and persistent God is.

★ Let them know you'll pray for them—then *pray* for them! Spiritual battles are best fought with spiritual weapons.

The truth is, most Christians hit points in their lives when they are tempted to go in the wrong direction. What God uses to bring them back is often another Christian friend who expresses genuine concern. Remember, God didn't sit idly by when the entire human race went its own way. He actively pursued His most important creation and made a way to bring them back. He told us the truth: we're sinners. But He didn't make it hard to return to the safety of His care. Even when we turn our back, He always loves us enough to stick close beside us. That is a good example to follow.

ULTIMATE CHOICE

"Will I be the type of friend who cares enough to tell his friends things they may not like to hear, or will I keep quiet when a friend starts heading in the wrong direction?"

BOYS . . .

. . . don't have the courage to say things that are true for fear of rejection.

MEN . . .

. . . love their friends enough to tell them the truth and point them back to the right direction.

THE WORD

Wounds from a friend are better than many kisses from an enemy.

PROVERBS 27:6

In the end, people appreciate frankness more than flattery.

PROVERBS 28:23

Most important of all, continue to show deep love for each other, for love covers a multitude of sins.

1 PETER 4:8

ACTION IDEA

Think through all of your close friends—especially those who perhaps used to be friends. Is there anyone whom you sense could benefit by some one-on-one genuine concern about the path he's headed down? If so, perhaps you're the one God is wanting to use to let him know.

18   *"Got a Minute?"*

Be your own man."

"Handle it like a man."

"A man's gotta do whatta man's gotta do."

"Stand tall, like a man."

When I hear those phrases I picture a solitary figure standing in the shadows. A man, alone with his thoughts, his life, his own decisions—and his misconceptions about what a man actually is!

Unfortunately, those types of phrases, though perhaps well-intentioned, only serve to pull men away from others. Certainly, there are times in a man's life when the final decision must be made alone; when he must do what he must do; when he must stand tall. But sadly, it's this type of macho attitude that gets us males in trouble.

You're heading into years when you'll be forced to make the toughest moral and life-altering decisions of your life. Things like:

* ✭ what elective classes you'll take in high school and college;

* ✭ what type of friends you'll hang with;

* ✭ what you'll think about church and the Christian faith;

* ✭ whether you'll allow friends—or your girlfriend— determine whether you'll have sex before marriage or not (if they aren't Christians, they'll likely not be advising virginity);

★ whether you'll be the type who takes the easy route, or whether you'll push yourself to be your best in all you do;

★ who your life mate will be;

★ what type of career you'll have throughout your twenties;

★ how much "freedom" you'll give yourself with your entertainment and alcohol (since drinking will be "legal" for you at 21).

These and dozens of other decisions are mostly made between the ages of fourteen and twenty-two.

Do you "be your own man" and make up your mind without the input of others? Does "standing tall" mean no one else's opinion matters? Just because you can "predict" what someone will say (like your parents), does that mean their opinion isn't worth anything?

It's tough for guys to ask advice. We get that pride thing going and we mistakenly feel that our manhood is in question if we ask anyone else what *they* would do. Asking advice isn't a sign of weakness, it's a sign of intelligence. Of course just asking for advice is only the first step. *Taking* the *best* advice is the second, and most important, step for a boy wanting to reach true manhood.

If you sent a thousand prisoners a questionnaire asking them if they knew the right way to go when they were younger but simply didn't want to follow the advice of family and friends, you'll likely get a 100 percent response in the affirmative. Most had people giving them the right advice, they just wouldn't listen.

Your current decisions aren't likely ones that will hold jail in the balance. They're (seemingly) a bit less life-changing. But are they really? Refer to that list on the previous page and you'll see that if you make bad choices in several of those areas, you could wind up in a lifetime of trouble. Wrong sexual choices, relationship choices, "freedom" choices, and friendship choices can potentially push you over the edge.

The Book of Proverbs has a lot to say about getting the right kind of advice. Here's one verse that sums it all up: "Fools think they need no advice, but the wise listen to others" (12:15).

The bottom line is getting wisdom in order to be wise. If you don't, the nameplate you'll wear will shine like a neon light in the forest: FOOL.

Wisdom is what is attained when experience (yours or someone else's) and God's truth are your teachers. What's great about wisdom is that if you're smart, you can own someone else's just by asking for it. Making bad choices and learning from your own experiences (while facing the consequences of them) doesn't have to be the only way to get wisdom.

There's just one step you must take: ask for it. Let's try an example. You're going through a huge dilemma, so you go to four people: your best friend, youth pastor, dad, and a teacher you like at school. You tell them what the problem is: "My girlfriend is pressuring me to have sex. You can imagine this makes it tough to try and stay pure. Help me sort through the upside and downside if we follow through with her plans."

Among all of the advice you'll get are responses that weigh the benefits with the costs.

Benefits:

★ It will feel good (for about fifteen or twenty minutes).

★ You won't have to wear the "virgin" name tag anymore.

★ When other guys find out (and they will), your "popularity" will increase.

★ It will show her you "love" her. (Check out the real definition of love in the dictionary and the Bible— 1 Corinthians 13:4–7.)

★ You'll be more experienced for the next girl.

Costs:

★ Once you lose it, you can never get it back.

★ You won't be able to give the gift of purity to your wife on your wedding night.

★ If you don't "handle things" correctly, she could get pregnant. (Are you ready to be a dad?)

★ If she wants to sleep with you, she's likely done it with other guys. And who knows whom *they* have slept with. Chances might be slim (though slightly possible) you'll become infected with HIV, but there are a few dozen other sexually transmitted diseases you could easily acquire. Even kissing a girl who's been around could give you herpes, a mouth disease you can *never* get rid of.

★ Is the guilt worth it?

★ It will be tougher to teach your kids the value of virginity before marriage if you weren't man enough to keep it. And who knows what type of diseases could infect them in twenty years. (In case you couldn't tell, your dad will give you this advice.)

★ Are you going to marry her? (Probably not.) Do you want some guy practicing on *your* future wife?

★ It's clearly not God's best. (Though it's a forgivable sin, the Bible most definitely condemns premarital sex.)

Would you have thought about these "benefits" and "costs" without taking the time to ask the four people their advice?

If you had the courage to seek this type of wisdom, you'd have more wisdom than you could have had by simply doing what you *felt* was right.

Not every choice in life needs the advice of four people, but the big choices certainly do. If you head to the right sources for wisdom, you'll be a man who will most definitely stand tall. You'll never be called a fool.

ULTIMATE CHOICE

"Will I be a Lone Ranger throughout my life, never seeking the wisdom of those who have walked before me, or will I drop the pride and seek after an abundance of counselors to insure victory?"

BOYS . . .

. . . believe the huge misconception that only "the strong, silent" type of guy is truly a man, and that asking for advice is a sign of weakness.

MEN . . .

. . . know that true wisdom and direction is found in the company of others who are wise; in others who only want God's best for their life—and yours.

THE WORD

Pride leads to arguments; those who take advice are wise.

PROVERBS 13:10

Get all the advice and instruction you can, and be wise the rest of your life.

PROVERBS 19:20

Oh, the joys of those who do not follow the advice of the wicked, or stand around with sinners, or join in with scoffers.

PSALM 1:1

ACTION IDEA

Have you been getting good advice lately? Think about the decisions you have to make in the next few weeks. To whom can you talk in order to get a different perspective on the decision you have to make?

19 *How to Treat a Lady*

I had a few college buddies who, when mealtime arrived, would pile their trays full of food, wander down to the end of one of the cafeteria dining rooms, face the hallway . . . and wait. When an unsuspecting female happened to head their direction, the rating game began.

"Six," one guy would say with a mouth full of Jell-O.

"Six? Are you blind?" said another between bites of mashed potatoes. "She's a three. What's your major . . . dog training?"

"Hey," another guy would say, "here comes that ten we saw yesterday."

"Ten?" one of the loudest guys yelled. "She's got to be at least a thirteen. Come sit with me, baby, I'm yours!"

And on it went—the daily rating game of every girl who was unlucky enough to walk close to our hallway.

Absolute hormonal idiots, that's what they were. But, of course, I didn't believe that strongly at the time. At first, I thought it was kinda funny—almost harmless. I'd been a Christian for less than a year and these guys were in my dorm. Their rating system had just one criteria: looks. That's *all* they cared about.

Thankfully, by midterm, the game was getting old. No, they didn't stop playing it, I simply woke up to the fact it was degrading and disgusting. God was showing me that these girls were human beings with mothers, fathers, and grandparents. While a few girls liked the attention (if they were tens), most were made to feel rotten. Why? Because a few guys had a warped sense of what it meant to be a man around females. Actually, they weren't men, they were just big boys.

You'll get all sorts of advice about females in your life—some will be good, some won't. The big question is, what will *you* believe about how to treat a lady?

Besides your spiritual life, this area needs close tracking like few others. Here is a truth: What you *think* about females is how you'll *behave* around them.

If you think girls are objects, you'll treat them that way. If you think a girl likes to be used and abused, that's what you'll do. If you think that it's all about looks, you'll eventually be playing the rating game. If you think that *real men* can do or say anything they want around females, get ready to be single for most of your life.

But if you think females are a special creation by God, deserving of your best behavior, you're on your way to a great life. Why? Because females have a built-in sense that lets them know if they're being cherished. They like being with men who cherish them a million times more than men who are idiots around them.

How do you treat a lady? Here are a few tips:

★ Since she's not one of the boys, try not to talk to her as if she were. That means no jokes she won't appreciate, bodily function noises, and comments about body parts.

★ Courtesy counts: Opening doors and allowing her to enter first (for everyone, not just the cute ones), standing when an adult lady enters the room (ask your dad about this one), listening to what they say (anything *small* that you think doesn't really matter—matters!).

★ While it's OK to want to spend time with females whom you judge to be more attractive, never, *never* make comments about looks or features in front of the girl—or with your friends. In case you didn't know, girls have a terrible time with their self-image. Hollywood, magazine covers, and billboards have created an unrealistic expectation about looks (especially for females, but for *you,* too), so they are *very* sensitive. Most are trying to look their best, so any hint of a put-down definitely communicates the wrong message. Fight the urge to say anything besides a compliment. Mom was right: "If you don't have anything nice to say—keep your yap shut."

One more thing: All of these tips on how to treat a lady goes triple for Mom. More than any other female in your life, she deserves your ultimate respect. How you treat your mom will communicate to your parents more than anything else how ready you are to spend time with females. Never a put-down, never a sneer, never an unkind remark, and you'll be trusted. And being trusted by females is what a man should be known for.

ULTIMATE CHOICE

"Will I go against what most guys do and treat females with respect because God has created them, or will I play the rating game while forgetting that they are human beings, not objects?"

BOYS . . .

. . . follow along with whatever their friends are doing, not wishing to stand out from the crowd to treat females with respect.

MEN . . .

. . . not only know how to treat females, they know how to think correctly about them as well.

THE WORD

Treat the older women as you would your mother, and treat the younger women with all purity as your own sisters.

1 TIMOTHY 5:2

ACTION IDEA

Examine your own thoughts, speech, and actions toward all of the females in your life. Are you treating them with respect? Are you doing the little things that should make them feel like the special creation of God that they are?

20 *Why Those Four Walls?*

I f I were to take a poll of 1,000 boys on what they think of church, the easy prediction is most would classify it as "boring." If their parents didn't make them go, they'd be sleeping or watching the "NBA Game of the Week."

I wasn't fortunate enough to be raised going to church. I slept and watched basketball. Perhaps you sometimes wish you weren't so "fortunate." Instead of a long lecture on the subject, I want you to stay closely tuned to the words, questions, and passages in this challenge. Because only men can understand what I'll be saying.

I've discovered that boys only want to be entertained for those one or two hours on Sunday morning; they only think about what they can *get* out of it. Men have learned that *getting* something out of church is important, but *giving* something back is why they're there.

Let me give you a few of the top reasons why it's essential to give back at church every chance you can.

It reminds me I don't have to be selfish all of the time. Like you, I'm self-centered by nature. That is, most of the time I'm thinking about how to make *my* life easy. Those four walls have given me a place to realize two of God's priorities: worshiping Him, and serving others. No "me" allowed. As the years go by, I realize how essential both of those priorities should be. Believe it or not, it actually gets boring always thinking about yourself. Focusing on God and serving others is a welcome change from me, me, me.

It reminds me I'm in a battle. I hate to admit it, but I fought for the enemy before I became a Christian. One of my high school friends told me he was considering Jesus Christ and he wondered what I thought about him becoming a Christian. I talked him out of it! When I became a follower of Christ two years later, he was one of the first guys I told. "Congratulations," he said, and I didn't see him again until my five-year reunion! By then, drugs had messed up his brain. He was what I could have been.

But Satan didn't give up on me after I said yes to Jesus. In fact, he continues to work hard at seeing me fall. He knows that if he can ruin my testimony by causing me to stumble, he will prevent others from even taking a passing glance at the Savior. This includes the most important people in my life—my own two boys.

Our lives share the message of Christ beyond what our words could ever do. You have likely felt the pressure to cave in and follow the ways of the world. If you have, then you know something of how intense the battle can be. Satan is real. His ability to continually plant thoughts into our heads is unquestioned. Paul was right when he identified where our battles are truly fought: "For we are not fighting against people made of flesh and blood, but against the evil rulers and authorities of the unseen world, against those mighty powers of darkness who rule this world, and against wicked spirits in the heavenly realms" (Ephesians 6:12).

The people, the message, the chance to serve and worship —all that occurs on Sunday morning reminds me whose side I'm on, and it helps equip me to do battle another week. If you're not experiencing opposition, if you don't know what I'm talking about, it's time to check and see whose army you're really serving.

I need someone else to help me understand and apply the Bible. I graduated from Bible college with a degree in Biblical Studies. I've read the New Testament about one hundred times and the Old Testament more than twenty. Yet I'm still amazed at all I don't know about God and the Bible. Without Sunday school and that thirty-minute sermon, I'd only be relying on *past* knowledge to get through *today*. I've learned that unless you hear from God—through other people who are hearing from God—you're not going to be equipped for the challenges you'll face in the near future.

When the children of Israel were in the wilderness for forty years, God fed them daily by sending manna and quail. Anything they tried to hoard was spoiled. Since God sees the big picture of my life, He knows my *future* spiritual needs far better than I. If I'm absent or mentally asleep at church, the very words I could have used to help me through a situation might never have been heard.

I need other friends who believe like I do. I'm not one of those Christians who thinks you shouldn't have non-Christian friends. I have plenty. They keep me sharp, I like them and I don't view them as targets. But if I didn't have a bunch of Christian friends, I'd have a tendency to think I'm the only Christian on the planet. Ever felt that way before? Sure you have! And when you do, it's tough to think like a Christian, let alone act like one.

Where can you find Christians whom you can befriend? Church is the best place I know. Fortunately, they're not *all* like you. There are "cool" Christians, "nerdy" Christians, and everything in between. God did good. He made different types of Christians for different types of people. You need church friends to encourage you in your faith.

I need to remember all that God has done. Communion reminds me of Christ's suffering. Baptism reminds me of His resurrection. The Christian "seasons"—Advent, Christmas, Lent, Easter—all remind me of important aspects of the faith that give me courage and joy. Hearing the testimonies from people who have received a recent or special touch by God reminds me that even though He may not be doing miracles in my own life right at the moment, He's still working overtime in the lives of others. The music often reminds me of God's character qualities that mean the most to me. The chance to give money back to Him reminds me that everything I have is just on loan—God owns it all. Hearing the Bible preached every week reminds me God loved me enough to leave me words that will light my path all the days of my life. When I'm not there, it's easy to forget about all this stuff.

The church is Christ's body. I'm a part of it. If I don't function, the whole body is hurt. I've mentioned this one before: God wants to use you. When He does, it's the funnest thing in the world. If you're not of a mind or in a place where God can use you, the Christian life becomes little more than mental beliefs to keep you out of hell.

Church is a great place to be used by God. But as you know, it's not the only place! God can use you at school, with a neighbor, at a homeless shelter, on the mission field, in your own home—wherever you are, God can use you. But if your head is only into yourself, you'll quit thinking about being used and concentrate on how to use others. Church is a great place to remember your life counts—it's needed to fulfill God's plan on earth, it's needed to bring others to a relationship with Christ, it's needed, it's needed, it's needed! (Get the picture?)

The point is, God knows we need "the church." And the best place to find the "the church" is church. Some have asked, "Is it possible to be a Christian and not go to church?" Sure, if you want to be a wimpy, self-centered believer.

If your church is boring, one way to solve that dilemma is to start looking at it through a different set of eyes. Ask God to show you ways to give of yourself while you're there—to remind you of things that will strengthen your faith.

That's what men do.

ULTIMATE CHOICE

"Do I know the difference between 'church' and 'the church' enough to want to be involved as God would have me?"

BOYS . . .

. . . only look for the entertainment value at church, and only seek what they can get out of church.

. . . look to what they can give to "the church."

_____ **THE WORD** _____

And let us not neglect our meeting together, as some people do, but encourage and warn each other, especially now that the day of his coming back again is drawing near.

HEBREWS 10:25

ACTION IDEA

Read these passages and answer these questions to get an even clearer picture.

✷ Why go to church?

—That we may "grow up" in Christ (Ephesians 4:15–16).
—To provide a place to worship (Psalm 48:1).
—To protect us from error (1 Timothy 4:1).
—To learn, fellowship, remember, and pray (Acts 2:42).
—To give (1 Corinthians 16:2).
—We're told to (Hebrews 10:25).

✷ Who started the church? Who can stop it? (Matthew 16:18)

✷ Who is the head? (Colossians 1:18)

✷ Who is always on our team? (Romans 8:34)

✷ Why are we different? (Ephesians 4:12)

21   Just One Peek

A s a naval academy midshipman, Jeff Gantar wanted to serve his country the way his father had in the Vietnam War and the way his grandfather had in World War II. He was proud the day the Navy accepted him and was looking forward to the military life. His grandfather even promised to give him his sword when he graduated from Annapolis. Motivated to succeed like few others, Jeff attacked his schoolwork like a bulldog.

Late one evening, before the biggest and most grueling test of his college career (Electrical Engineering 301), another classmate brought in some papers that looked exactly like what Jeff thought the test would be. *But this couldn't be the test,* he reasoned. So like hundreds of other classmates, he used the papers as a basis to study from. The next morning when the tests were handed out, Jeff couldn't believe what he saw. What he had studied the night before and what he was looking at in front of him were the same papers!

At that instant, Jeff had a choice to make. He could walk to the front of the class and admit what happened to his instructor. Or he could do what more than 200 other midshipmen did—act like nothing was wrong and take the test.

The moment he started filling out the answers, he knew he'd be breaking the Honor Concept by cheating. He knew what was right. Naval academy midshipmen should have enough integrity and honor not to cheat. He anguished for a few moments, looked around to see what others were doing, and took the test.

Eventually, however, his conscience would not let him keep quiet any longer. More than a year later, he and a handful of other midshipmen, just a few short months away from graduation and assignments as naval officers, came clean. Those who admitted they cheated were kicked out. Those who were implicated, but lied, and dozens of others who were never called to account for their actions, are now officers in the U.S. Navy.

Cheating is pretending you know something you don't. It's taking an unfair advantage so you can obtain for free what others have earned through superior intelligence or harder work. Not many boys would admit it's the right thing, but not many can say they haven't done it.

Jeff Gantar cheated, admitted it (eventually), and paid the consequences. He's sorry for what he did, he's sorry for the consequences, but he's happy that he regained his honor. (His gripping story is in a book called *A Question of Honor,* Zondervan Publishing House, 1996.)

When you face the choice to cheat on your schoolwork, the consequences you face if you're caught will not be as dramatic. That's why so many still cheat. They think it's not that big a deal, and, of course, "everyone does it."

I won't moralize by asking, "If everyone jumped off a cliff, would you?" But I will challenge you by asking a few questions:

★ What do you want to be known for, getting a good grade point average or having roving eyes?

★ Is honesty a higher value than false accomplishment?

★ Would your parents rather you worked hard and take what you earned, or do they only care about "the grade"?

Your true character shines through when no one else is around to make sure you do the right thing. Like Jeff Gantar, you'll wrestle with moments of decision that will communicate to you—and God—what you're really made of on the inside. The Bible, this book, your parents, and your youth leader won't be there. It'll simply be you and your own thoughts about what is truly important.

What *is* important to you?

ULTIMATE CHOICE

"Will I be the type of male who consistently chooses long-lasting character over momentary 'achievement,' or will I believe that cheating and lying is so accepted by most people that it just doesn't matter?"

BOYS . . .

. . . take the easy way out and cheat, lying to themselves and others that it doesn't matter.

MEN . . .

. . . hold on to honesty and honor no matter what the consequences because what's on the inside is what counts in life.

THE WORD

But the good soil represents honest, good-hearted people who hear God's message, cling to it, and steadily produce a huge harvest.

LUKE 8:15

Pray for us, for our conscience is clear and we want to live honorably in everything we do.

HEBREWS 13:18

ACTION IDEA

Decide today what kind of male you want to be. Decide what you want to be known for. Decide to take the path of honesty and integrity.

22

What Life Really Promises

ifteen-year-old Jeremy and his girlfriend went for a walk with his young nieces one Monday night. They stopped by my house, and we made small talk for a few minutes. He had just made a commitment to Christ at a weekend retreat we returned home from the day before. After saying good-bye, they headed on their way. Five minutes later, Jeremy lay on the pavement, hit from behind by a drunk driver. Less than an hour later I listened in stunned silence as an emergency room doctor had the unpleasant task of announcing to his parents their son was dead. Three days later I performed a memorial service for Jeremy amidst dozens of his family and friends who had but one question on their minds: Why?

I met James his senior year in high school. A sensitive young man who loved God with all of his heart, he talked of his faith, trucks, school, and college plans. Though normal in most every way, James wasn't physically the same as all of his classmates. He had been born with his eyes almost touching his ears. The front of his head was oversized. Hair grew in all of the wrong places on his face. By the time I got to know him, he'd had over ten surgeries to correct his abnormality. Another ten would be needed. I never heard James ask "why?"

Pete had a hard time fitting in with others from school. Most hated him because he was so socially inept. After a year of just trying to be his friend, Pete shared with me that when he was in grade school, his uncle had repeatedly raped him. Thoughts that he was a homosexual led to suicide attempts. He was going to church, but people there didn't treat him any differently than the rest. He was too busy trying to survive to even think "why?"

The longer you live on earth, the more tragic people and situations you'll witness. If you don't say these words out loud, you'll think them: *God, where were You when this was going on? You're all-powerful, You're all-knowing—You could have done something! Why didn't You?*

Bad stuff happens. And if it hasn't happened to you, it probably will.

A relationship with a girl will hurt you to the core.

You'll break your arm before the football season of your senior year.

Your mom will get cancer. After suffering through dozens of treatments that make her violently sick, she'll die a slow and seemingly cruel death.

Perhaps it will be you with the disease. Or a sibling. Maybe *your* child will one day face an illness the doctors can't fix.

Life has a tendency to progress at a normal pace, then BAM! Something happens that will be worse than anything you've ever faced. If it happened today, what would you do? What will you think? Does God get the blame? Or will you turn to Him like a trusted friend? Will Christ's death on the cross have any meaning for you, or will you shake your fist in the air and tell Him He isn't worthy of your love and obedience? Will you be tempted to think He doesn't even exist?

For some odd reason, many Christians have a tendency to think that once they trust God with their lives, they're suddenly immune to the bad side effects from our fallen world. That since God obviously loves them *more,* He'll protect them from anything bad that could happen.

Some Christians have been misinformed. They didn't read the promise direct from the mouth of Jesus Christ. "I have told you all this so that you may have peace in me. Here on earth you will have many trials and sorrows. But take heart, because I have overcome the world" (John 16:33).

While God and His angels have likely protected you and me from countless tragedies, sometimes He allows us to face them. Jesus didn't heal every person while He walked the earth; that wasn't His mission. And it's obvious He doesn't heal every Christian on earth today. So if He doesn't always "fix" the "bad situations" in life, please don't conclude He doesn't love you or isn't just as committed to you as when life was rosey.

There will be a lot of great times you'll experience during your short stay on this planet. You'll also plod through a lot of boring, ordinary days. But neither of these are promised. What *is* promised are "many trials and sorrows." Some will face more than their share, others less. While a few of the trials and sorrows will be the self-inflicted variety ("you'll reap what you have sown"), most will come out of nowhere. You won't be able to point a finger to anyone in blame. Nor should you. Remember, God has your hairs numbered. He knows when a sparrow falls from the earth. You are of much greater value than a sparrow.

ULTIMATE CHOICE

"When bad times occur, will I shake my fist at God, telling Him He's unkind and unfair, or will I take the bad with the good, recognizing that while God has promised trials on earth, He's also secured my eternity through Jesus?"

BOYS . . .

. . . believe life should only be filled with good times and an absence of pain.

MEN . . .

. . . realize the truth behind this fallen world—that Christians aren't immune to the bad side effects of sin, but that God promises peace in the midst of the trials that will inevitably come.

THE WORD

"When the world hates you, remember it hated me before it hated you. The world would love you if

you belonged to it, but you don't. I chose you to
come out of the world, and so it hates you."

JOHN 15:18–19

God blesses the people who patiently endure
testing. Afterward they will receive the crown of life
that God has promised to those who love him.

JAMES 1:12

ACTION IDEA

Take a few minutes to think about how you would
respond to God if something terrible happened to you or
someone you love. Have this important issue thought through
before it happens. Or if you're facing a tragedy or difficult trial
right now, examine how you are responding to God.

23

Contented as You Wanna Be

A t what age do you think you'll learn that enough is enough?

Enough possessions.
Enough status.
Enough pretty women to be with.
Enough cars to drive.
Enough CDs in your collection.
Enough athletic accomplishments to prove to everyone you're good.

Many males never learn. Whatever their eyes gaze upon or TV commercials say they "need," they want. They'll work overtime (at the expense of their family); they'll go in debt to purchase what they want—now!; they'll let their eyes gawk at other females, thinking they could "move up" to a newer model. What they have is never enough because there's always something better, bigger, prettier, faster.

They think,

The applause will be louder if . . .
My dad will be even more proud of me if . . .
I'll be happier with . . .

I've been talking about other guys, but I know that *I'm* not immune to this same temptation. You won't be either. Of course, who can blame us? When we're young we're rewarded when we have a better car, a prettier girlfriend, more money in our wallet, and nicer clothes. As we get older, people still notice these things, but a bigger house, a boat, or a promotion are things we'll desire—things we *think* we need in order to look good and feel good about ourselves.

Wanting better stuff isn't always evil. But caving in to the pressure to move up the ladder in possessions is like a hamster on a round treadmill. You think you're getting someplace, but you're actually not—and it looks *really* funny. All it does is prove the apostle John true when he said, "Stop loving this evil world and all that it offers you, for when you love the world, you show that you do not have the love of the Father in you. For the world offers only the lust for physical pleasure, the lust for everything we see, and pride in our possessions. These are not from the Father. They are from this evil world. And this world is fading away, along with everything it craves. But if you do the will of God, you will live forever" (1 John 2:15–17).

So what is the will of God when it comes to handling correctly all that the world wants to dangle in front of your face?

Contentment. Being truly satisfied with what you have.

It doesn't mean you quit working hard to improve your life. But acquiring *more* doesn't become the all-consuming passion that many males (notice I didn't say "men") are addicted to. This type of addiction is tough to break. Once you've known the feelings of pride you get when you've shown the world you can own something "better," once you've heard the applause and "way-to-go's" from people you want to impress, you've ceased trying to please the One whom you should be impressing: God.

Why is this a problem? Because "this world is fading away, along with everything it craves" (1 John 2:17, TNLB).

Millions of males are in the process of destroying their children, their marriages, their spiritual lives because they haven't learned the secret of contentment. The real issue for men is fear. They think, *If I don't have enough _____, my dad, my wife (girlfriend), and my friends won't think I've got what it takes.* For many males, this is a fear that grips them around the throat their entire lives. And it's a fear they pass down to their sons, as well.

As you'll remember, we've talked about fear already. The only way to destroy fear is to look it in the eye and recognize the truth. The writer to the Hebrews hit the nail on the head when he compared the love of money with the fear of not getting attention from others. He said, "Stay away from the love of money; be satisfied with what you have. For God has said, 'I will never fail you. I will never forsake you'" (Hebrews 13:5).

If you knew that the God of the universe was always with you, there would be nothing to fear and no one to impress, right? You'd jump off of the "possession treadmill" as fast as you could. And once you were off of that treadmill, you'd realize how ridiculous everyone looks running so fast as they go nowhere besides deeper into their fears.

Are you ready to jump? Now's the time before you get too accustomed to that treadmill of fear and discontentment.

ULTIMATE CHOICE

"Will I pursue the pride of ownership on what my friends or the world says is important, or will I pursue pleasing God and being content with what I have?"

BOYS . . .

. . . foolishly think more and better possessions will fill their life with enough to get noticed by others.

MEN . . .

. . . work hard to improve their lives, but know that only a heart filled with contentment and a knowledge of God's presence can truly satisfy—in this life and the next.

THE WORD

The fear of the LORD leads to life: Then one rests content, untouched by trouble.
PROVERBS 19:23, NIV

I am not saying this because I am in need, for I have learned to be content whatever the circumstances. I know what it is to be in need, and I know what it is to have plenty. I have learned the secret of

being content in any and every situation, whether
well fed or hungry, whether living in plenty or in
want.

PHILIPPIANS 4:11–12, NIV

ACTION IDEA

What things give you the most positive "attention" from others? Do you *live* to hear from others how cool you are because of a talent or possession? If so, talk to another Christian man and together figure out a way to get closer to God's ideal of contentment.

24 Controlling the Beast of Anger

Someone famous in history once said, "We have met the enemy, and the enemy is us."

And then there is the familiar motherly phrase, "You're your own worst enemy."

What about the Bible? "A person without self-control is as defenseless as a city with broken-down walls" (Proverbs 25:28). A different version says, "Whoever has no rule over his own spirit is like a city broken down, without walls (NKJV).

I could copy this verse in a dozen other translations, and I could find hundreds of other quotes that talk about us as our biggest problem, and they would all point back to one thing: *We* have the potential to be the beast! *We* can be the enemy— and our own worst one at that! The devil may plant thoughts, he may even be arranging circumstances in his battle plan to destroy our lives, but we make the final choice to allow the voice of darkness to control our actions.

There are many areas where men become like a city with broken-down walls: spending money, bragging, cheating, humor, what we watch when we have a TV remote in our hands. Two areas, however, are the most deadly to our pursuit of a manhood that honors God: anger and lust. I'm going to talk first about anger. In the next chapter we'll handle the tricky topic of lust.

Have you ever noticed why someone gets "raising their voice" angry? They have lost control. And people hate to lose control! Your dad perhaps raises his voice when he wants to control you. His boss yells at him when he wants to control him. When you want to control your little brother or someone at school, you raise your voice. Sharp words spoken loudly send a message: "You're not doing what *I* want, so you better do it now or I'll raise my voice again—or worse!" Coaches, teachers, even youth leaders use the same tactic. Mostly for good reason.

While some kinds of anger are good, there is another kind that leaves us open to satanic influence. Paul said, "And 'don't sin by letting anger gain control over you.' Don't let the sun go down while you are still angry, for anger gives a mighty foothold to the Devil" (Ephesians 4:26–27).

There are dozens of other passages that talk about anger, and if you think you have a problem with uncontrolled anger, you ought to begin to memorize a few of them (look in a concordance). The point is that anger opens the door. It allows the enemy to come inside the walls and destroy you from within.

The answer is to give up. That's right, give up your belief that you always need to be in control. The truth is, you'll never be in total control—that's God's job. When you face a situation where you're tempted to vent your anger, remember that it's your job to control yourself and it's God's job to control the circumstances. It truly is the only way to keep Satan from destroying you from within.

Let's say a referee makes an awful call against you. It not only makes you look bad, it costs the team. When a ref makes a call, it's nearly always final. You can yell and swear and give him a look that you wish could kill, but it won't change his mind. All anger does is get your thoughts off of the game. For many players, it takes them out of the contest completely. A number of years ago, major league pitcher David Cone took a throw from the first baseman as he ran to cover first. He thought he beat the runner to the bag, but the ump called the runner safe. David went ballistic! He ran over to the ump to argue the call (as if the ump would change it just because David got mad). While he kept yelling, two other runners circled the bases and scored. His uncontrolled anger in the heat of competition not only made him look stupid on national TV, but it cost his team the game.

Give up your ideas that you can control situations and start realizing the only thing you should control is you. Otherwise, Mom will be right: You will be your own worst enemy.

ULTIMATE CHOICE

"Will I allow my lack of self-control to vent itself through anger, or will I choose to keep the walls in my life strong by giving up my desire for control and allowing God to do His job?"

BOYS . . .

. . . do not recognize the need to keep their temper under control.

MEN . . .

. . . know that God is in control and that self-control in the area of anger allows Satan to only knock at the door—not come in.

THE WORD

You should also know this, Timothy, that in the last days there will be very difficult times. For people will love only themselves and their money. They will be boastful and proud, scoffing at God, disobedient to their parents, and ungrateful. They will consider nothing sacred. They will be unloving and unforgiving; they will slander others and <u>have no self-control</u>; they will be cruel and have no interest in what is good. They will betray their friends, be reckless, be puffed up with pride, and love pleasure rather than God. They will act as if they are religious, but they will reject the power that could make them godly. You must stay away from people like that.

2 TIMOTHY 3:1–5 (EMPHASIS ADDED)

> *So make every effort to apply the benefits of these promises to your life. Then your faith will produce a life of moral excellence. A life of moral excellence leads to knowing God better. <u>Knowing God leads to self-control. Self-control leads to patient endurance,</u> and patient endurance leads to godliness. Godliness leads to love for other Christians, and finally you will grow to have genuine love for everyone. The more you grow like this, the more you will become productive and useful in your knowledge of our Lord Jesus Christ.*
>
> 2 PETER 1:5–8 (EMPHASIS ADDED)

ACTION IDEA

Since self-control in the area of anger takes practice, start identifying what makes you lose your temper and choose to build your self-control wall strong so you can be a man who doesn't give the devil a way into his life.

25

It's the Thought That Counts

A number of years ago, I was lamenting to my pastor about an area of my life that I couldn't get under control: my thought life. I said, "I've memorized verses, I'm careful about what I set my eyes on, I try not to look when a pretty woman passes by. But my mind still goes haywire way too often." Then I hit him with the question I knew he had the answer to. After all, he was wiser, older, much more spiritual than I, and had a very pretty wife. I asked, "When does this lust thing start to wind down?" I wasn't prepared for his response.

"It doesn't."

"Excuse me. Do you mean to say I'm always going to be fighting this battle?"

"As long as you're on planet earth, the enemy will seek to cause you to stumble at your weakest point. For most guys, it's lust."

Today, I'm older, wiser; I've read the Bible another half-dozen times, memorized more verses, talked to tons of men about this issue, been to hundreds of church services, written twenty books; and I've discovered . . . he was right! That's why I can say with confidence that sexual lust will be an issue you'll have to tackle every day of your life.

Having said all of that, you'll be surprised to hear me say there *is* hope. You *can* win a high percentage of your battles. And God *does* come to your aid whenever He's asked. Here's how it can be done:

Decide today that you won't be like others—those whose heads constantly turn, those whose eyes linger a bit too long at the grocery store magazine rack, and those who attempt to catch as much skin as they can in TV and movies.

This will be a tough choice, because you'll not get too many people patting you on the back when your eyes stay focused straight ahead. It's natural to look, perhaps even "normal." After all, it's a known fact that males are more visually-oriented than females. And fighting that urge to look —especially if you know you won't get "caught"—is definitely going above and beyond. But that's what *men* do. In a very real sense, they look *above* and they look *beyond*. They know "the world offers only the lust for physical pleasure, the lust for everything we see, and pride in our possessions. These are not from the Father. They are from this evil world. And this world is fading away, along with everything it craves. But if you do the will of God, you will live forever" (1 John 2:16–17).

While you're working on this, remember: As with everything, progress, not perfection, is what God wants to see. Keeping your heart and mind focused on purity five out of seven days a week is much better than one out of seven.

Progress.

Learn what it means to take a thought captive. Lust is a mind thing. The sexual battle begins within the deep inner recesses of a man's heart that only he—and God—can see. In truth, lust is actually the sin of coveting—wanting something that doesn't belong to you. The world rarely acknowledges lust's danger, but Jesus knew. The Savior understood that unbridled lust leaves a man just one small step away from even greater levels of sexual sin. "You have heard that the law of Moses says, 'Do not commit adultery.' But I say, anyone who even looks at a woman with lust in his eye has already committed adultery with her in his heart" (Matthew 5:27–28). And once the heart is committed—or open—to adultery (*fornication* is the term if you're not married), actions are sure to follow.

Paul said, "and we take captive every thought to make it obedient to Christ" (2 Corinthians 10:5, NIV). Capturing lustful thoughts and making them obedient to Christ is no easy task, especially in our sexually-saturated society. But think of it this way: If you were a general for the good guys, and the bad guys kept coming over to your camp to try to take you prisoner, what would you do? You'd either kill that enemy or capture him. A general knows when an enemy has entered his camp *(the lustful thought)*. The uniform is different and the bad guy's goals are different, too *(to keep you in bondage to sin)*. He's trying to take territory that doesn't belong to him *(your heart and mind belong to God)*.

It is Satan's goal to make males slaves to sexual sin. He enters a Christian male's camp by way of his thoughts—often when they are first young boys. Many boys and older males don't put up a fight. They simply throw up their hands and surrender. But *your goal* isn't giving in to the forces of darkness who want to destroy. Your goal is obedience to Jesus Christ so that you're ready to fight in *His* army! And in case you forgot— it's the *winning* army. Don't give up! Take that thought captive —even if it tries to enter your camp fifty times a day. Even if it's entering fifty times an hour (which for a lot of us guys, it does). "In the name of Jesus, if you take one step closer, you're my prisoner. Now, get out of my camp!"

Don't let sexual sin become progressive. For most teenage guys, lust that has begun in the mind slowly works its way out in so-called harmless forms of behavior: pornography and masturbation. But even this illicit enticement gets old. Premarital sex—or taking a girl as far as she'll let you—is sure to follow. Guaranteed. And if you've made a "True Love Waits" commitment, count on being tested in this area—perhaps relentlessly. So much so you'll feel like giving up.

Maybe you've already given up and acted on your lusts; you've crossed the line in your actions with a girl. In either case, there is a place where all men can go to start over: the foot of the Cross.

We know that Jesus was tempted in every way, yet without sin (Hebrews 4:15). That means He experienced the power of sexual lust. He was shown that road and said no to it. If He lives in your heart, He can now come to your help so you can say no to it too. Ask Him for it.

P.S. There is much that can be said in this area. Space only allows me to touch on the bottom-line issue of the thought life. I've written other books on the subject. If you're in junior high, *Getting Ready for the Guy/Girl Thing* is the book for you. If you're in high school, pick up *What Hollywood Won't Tell You about Sex, Love, and Dating* (both with Regal Books).

ULTIMATE CHOICE

"Will I be a male who allows the enemy access to my thought life, or will I be a man who captures those thoughts of lust and takes them prisoner?"

BOYS . . .

. . . give up when the enemy enters the camp of their minds. They are not certain they want to have a clean thought life, nor do they trust the power of God to help them conquer impure thoughts.

MEN . . .

. . . know that this area can destroy them—both now and in the future—and take steps to protect their minds from being overrun with lustful thoughts.

THE WORD

So put to death the sinful, earthly things lurking within you. Have nothing to do with sexual sin, impurity, lust, and shameful desires. Don't be greedy for the good things of this life, for that is idolatry.

COLOSSIANS 3:5

With the Lord's authority let me say this: Live no longer as the ungodly do, for they are hopelessly confused. Their closed minds are full of darkness; they are far away from the life of God because they have shut their minds and hardened their hearts against him. They don't care anymore about right

*and wrong, and they have given themselves over to
immoral ways. Their lives are filled with all kinds of
impurity and greed. But that isn't what you were
taught when you learned about Christ.*

EPHESIANS 4:17–20

ACTION IDEA

If you're struggling with lustful thoughts, chances are,
other guys are too. Find a couple of other guys with commit-
ments to purity who will help keep your life free from enemy
intruders.

26 *The "L" Word*

CAUTION: This reading has an "edge" to it. If you're not prepared to be honestly challenged about your work habits, skip to the next reading.

Have you ever been accused of being lazy? Do your parents give you grief over your sleeping habits? Are paying jobs the kind of things *other guys* do because they don't have a life?

You may not know it, but one of a parent's worst nightmares is to have a lazy son—someone who doesn't comprehend the value of good, honest work. They fear it so much that they start to put you to work as soon as they can. Small chores escalate in degree of difficulty in direct proportion to how much you're growing. That is, the bigger you are, the more work they'll get out of you.

"Unfair," you say? Actually, it's the best thing in the world they can do for you. They know that once you leave home, you'll need to eat. (Are you aware that one day you'll actually be *paying for* and *making* your own food?) And they're probably acquainted with the following passages:

> *Even while we were with you, we gave you this rule: "Whoever does not work should not eat."*
>
> 2 THESSALONIANS 3:10

> *A lazy person sleeps soundly—and goes hungry.*
>
> PROVERBS 19:15

> *But you, lazybones, how long will you sleep? When will you wake up? I want you to learn this lesson: A little extra sleep, a little more slumber, a little folding of the hands to rest—and poverty will pounce on you like a bandit; scarcity will attack you like an armed robber.*
>
> PROVERBS 6:9–11

While your parents are busy obeying God by getting you ready to care for yourself, what are you doing?

Sleeping? Complaining? Arguing? Tuning them out while you tune in the TV? Doing your job half-way, just enough to get by?

The truth is, your attitude about work in these early days of heading toward manhood may determine your future happiness here on earth. I'm hitting this hard (and sounding a bit like a parent) because a poor attitude about work is incredibly widespread among teenage guys. Does this mean that you have to love working as much as pizza and videos? No, but it shouldn't be something to dread either—no matter how hard the task. Why? Because to *live* is to work.

So . . . what kind of job are you doing as you're living and working? If you're giving work—any work—only half of your effort, choosing when you'll push your abilities to the limit, that's the kind of man you could end up becoming: half a man. Half effort . . . half quality . . . half pay . . . half a sense of accomplishment. Count on it. (Have I got your attention?)

Will you be the type of worker who only lives for lunches and weekends, or will you be among the few who take pride in their work—*and does it as unto the Lord.*

Those last seven words are the key—perhaps for your entire life. Do you work for you, or do you work for the Lord? If you work for you, you can choose to perhaps "get by," but if your attitude is that you're working for God—in everything you do—your effort, quality, sense of accomplishment, and probably your pay will multiply. You'll feel good too!

Work and laziness aren't simply choices as to how you spend a few hours of your life. They are choices that reflect your true attitude about God and the place He's put you in.

If you're a student and you're only doing your homework half way, you're telling God you think He was foolish to put you in that school or that class.

If your parents have given you chores to do around the house, and you do them just good enough to get your allowance, you're telling God you're not ready for more important work later in life. (He's testing and preparing you for greater work that He wants you to do.)

If you're flipping burgers, throwing papers, bucking hay, pulling weeds, mowing lawns, selling shoes . . . and you've got that get-by attitude going, plan on never moving up to greater responsibility. (Can you say, "minimum wage"?)

As you are assigned jobs to do, the best way to do them—whatever they are—is as if you're doing them for God Himself. Remember, whether you realize it or not, YOU ARE!

ULTIMATE CHOICE

"Will I do my work the way *I* want to do it, or will my attitude be that I'm doing all the work I do for the King of Kings and Lord of Lords?"

BOYS . . .

. . . do their work as quickly and with the least amount of effort as possible.

MEN . . .

. . . do all of their work and tasks to please the One who gave them their work, as if it will be inspected by God Himself.

THE WORD

But you shouldn't be so concerned about perishable things like food. Spend your energy seeking the eternal life that I, the Son of Man, can give you.

JOHN 6:27

> *Lazy people don't even cook the game they catch, but the diligent make use of everything they find.*
>
> PROVERBS 12:27

> *Never be lazy in your work, but serve the Lord enthusiastically.*
>
> ROMANS 12:11

ACTION IDEA

In the next few tasks you do, check your attitude about how you're doing them. Are you working to "get it done," or are you working as if Jesus Christ were standing next to you, waiting to check the quality of your work? (Because He is!)

27

A Leader Worth Following

Most guys are afraid of being a leader. It's easier to follow someone else, so that's what they do. As you've gathered so far, much about becoming a Christian man means launching out, away from your comfort zones into unknown territory. Leadership even more so. So I'm not going to let you off too easily. Why? The world needs more Christian men who will learn what it means to use their God-given personality and skills to be a leader.

Leadership, however, is work. The chance for failure is higher. The adage is true: If you don't do anything, you can't do anything wrong.

I'm going to take you on a quick journey through the life of a man named John Mark. When I'm finished, you'll see how his life relates to yours.

John Mark (better known as Mark) was a young kid when he joined the apostle Paul on his first missionary journey. Tradition says that the last supper (Luke 22) and the amazing gathering of the disciples at Pentecost (Acts 2) was held in his mother's home. That means Mark had not only seen Jesus, he likely saw the powerful way in which God was using the early believers. We first meet Mark after Peter's miraculous escape from prison. "After a little thought, he [Peter] went to the home of Mary, the mother of John Mark, where many were gathered for prayer" (Acts 12:12).

So now, young Mark has not only seen Jesus, witnessed Pentecost, but while he was praying with a few other believers

—probably for Peter—who should show up at the door? Peter! Can you say . . . *miracle!* Mark is stoked. He's ready to do *anything* to serve such a miraculous God. When Paul and Barnabas announce they're getting on a boat and heading west to tell the pagans about Jesus, Mark signs up. But something happens. As soon as he gets off the boat, he wants to go home. "Now Paul and those with him left Paphos by ship for Pamphylia, landing at the port town of Perga. There John Mark left them and returned to Jerusalem" (Acts 13:13).

Why did Mark decide to head back home? We don't know exactly, but we do know his departure wasn't because of illness or injury. It was intentional. "After some time Paul said to Barnabas, 'Let's return to each city where we previously preached the word of the Lord, to see how the new believers are getting along.' Barnabas agreed and wanted to take along John Mark. But Paul disagreed strongly, since John Mark had deserted them in Pamphylia and had not shared in their work. Their disagreement over this was so sharp that they separated. Barnabas took John Mark with him and sailed for Cyprus. Paul chose Silas, and the believers sent them off, entrusting them to the Lord's grace" (Acts 15:36–40).

The great apostle Paul didn't want to take another chance that John Mark would wimp out again. Barnabas, the man whose name means "encourager," saw something in Mark besides blood ties (they were cousins) and knew that he deserved another chance. The rift between Paul and Barnabas was so tense, they parted ways. About twenty years later, ol' Mark reappeared. Paul was languishing in a Roman prison, writing letters like crazy, when he said this: "Aristarchus, who is in prison with me, sends you his greetings, and so does Mark, Barnabas's cousin. And as you were instructed before, make Mark welcome if he comes your way" (Colossians 4:10).

Mark wasn't in prison *with* Paul, he had come to help. At some point in time, Paul and Mark were reunited. What likely happened was that Mark finally proved himself to Paul. Paul became convinced that Mark had what it took. Three years later, Paul was back in another Roman prison, this time writing what proved to be his last letter (about A.D. 67). He ended his second letter to Timothy by saying, "Only Luke is with me. Bring Mark with you when you come, for he will be helpful to me" (2 Timothy 4:11).

From deserter to helper, John Mark had redeemed his earlier mistakes and become one of the leaders in all of Christianity. Peter dictated his account of the life of Jesus to Mark in the book of the same name, forever reminding the world of a young man's struggle to be the leader he was meant to be.

No doubt Mark knew he had failed when he left the missionary journey. But he didn't let it convince himself he was a *failure*. He learned that when you make a mistake—even a big one—you brush yourself off and move ahead.

Every man who has made attempts at leadership has failed. Every one. Whether it's in the church or with their families, men make errors in judgment. It's a pride bruiser, so many men, instead of risking their ego, take the easy way out and "let someone else do it." They let someone else organize that food drive. They let someone else pray. They let someone else volunteer to teach Sunday school. They let someone else take the responsibility to teach their family about the Lord.

Have you ever struggled with wanting to be a leader, failing, and then wondering if you'll always be a follower?

Contrary to what you think, real leaders aren't the popular, good-looking, athletic guys at your school. True leadership is letting God know you're available for anything—even if it means stepping out of your comfort zone. It's waking each day with the same statement Isaiah said to God, "Here am I, send me!" It's knowing that *you* are God's man.

Mark found out that being a leader didn't mean being the one in charge *or* being perfect. He failed miserably. No one would have been surprised if he had retired to tending sheep or fishing for the rest of his life, melting into obscurity. But he picked himself up and went for it. Even Paul's lack of faith in him didn't detour him from wanting to serve God. I heard a speaker once say, "I want to do something for God, even if it's making mistakes."

Does God want *you* to be a leader? Though I don't know you, I can answer with confidence, without a doubt! He's been developing shy guys into confident men for centuries. All He's looking for is someone who is available. What you need after a willing heart is an attitude that communicates you won't quit.

There are many different ways you can lead out over the next few years. You can

★ be a consistent example (I didn't say perfect);

★ help those who are tempted to throw their faith aside, encouraging them to finish the race;

★ gather a few guys together at school and begin to pray for your friends who don't know the Lord;

★ organize your youth group to help clean up a widow's yard;

★ ask your youth leader what you can do to help, saying no job is too small or too large;

★ be the one who prays at meals at your home.

Yes, you'll occasionally fail, but that's part of the learning process. Once you've made a mistake, then you've been educated. That is just one mistake you won't have to make again! Go ahead. Take a chance. Lead out.

ULTIMATE CHOICE

"Will I resign myself to being a follower of the crowd while I'm trying to be a follower of Jesus, or will I begin to stand tall and lead?"

BOYS . . .

. . . follow whoever is leading at the particular moment.

MEN . . .

. . . stand firm in their convictions and attempt to be the influencer instead of the influenced.

THE WORD

Don't let anyone think less of you because you are young. Be an example to all believers in what you teach, in the way you live, in your love, your faith, and your purity.

1 TIMOTHY 4:12

The members of the council were amazed when they saw the boldness of Peter and John, for they could see that they were ordinary men who had had no special training. They also recognized them as men who had been with Jesus.

ACTS 4:13

When the church at Jerusalem heard what had happened, they sent Barnabas to Antioch. When he arrived and saw this proof of God's favor, he was filled with joy, and he encouraged the believers to stay true to the Lord. Barnabas was a good man, full of the Holy Spirit and strong in faith. And large numbers of people were brought to the Lord. Then Barnabas went on to Tarsus to find Saul.

ACTS 11:22–25

ACTION IDEA

What one small area at your church or in your home can you volunteer to take the lead with?

28 *In My Weakness, He Is Strong*

Do you have an ear wing-span that would rival any B-52? Are you skinny enough to hide behind the school flag pole?

Have you ever said something so stupid in class that everyone—including the teacher—laughed *at* you (as opposed to *with* you)?

In junior high, because I was growing so fast, it seemed like I *always* had high-water pants. Add that to my white socks and old Keds tennis shoes, and I looked pretty geeky. In high school, it *always* seemed like I had a few new "friends" on my face each morning. I walked the halls in fear that people would want to stop me and play connect the dots on my face with their pen. In my late teens and early twenties, the unthinkable occurred: I started to get a receding hairline! (Today, it's in full-blown retreat.)

You know kids at school who are overweight, who always have bad hair days, who look like their grandma dressed them, who are consistently saying the wrong thing, who haven't showered in a few days—it seems that nearly everyone has minor to major "imperfections" that could be pointed out. Some imperfections can be helped, but most can't. You're born with that big nose. Or because your mom works and your dad moved away when you were eight, no one ever taught you Basic Grooming 101. Or because your dad's really quiet you've never learned how to express your-self in a group of people. You may seem like a social doofus

110

when you're really a pretty cool guy on the inside, but you just can't seem to make anyone see the real you. *(Breath.)*

The truth is: *Everyone* was created with a few minor to major imperfections. Something is either "wrong" with your body, or you simply haven't learned the essential social graces. And you know, if you *do* have any imperfections, God didn't mean for them to happen or wasn't aware of them, so you're a freak of nature.

Umm, did you see anything wrong with that last sentence?

Nothing catches God by surprise. He's not punishing you or others for anything you've done wrong if you have a minor (or major) imperfection that makes you look a bit different from others. In fact, to God, there's no such thing as imperfections. No matter how life or genetics "deforms" a human being, He can still use that person to do incredible things. You see, God has the ability to look at the big picture. He knows that life on planet earth is a drop in the bucket as it relates to eternity, so He doesn't sweat the small stuff. (I'm not sure He sweats at all, actually.)

If it's *small stuff* to God, should it be *big stuff* to you? Absolutely not! Anything small to God should be small to you.

While the Bible doesn't get too specific about the "imperfections" of those whom God used, it mentions a few:

★ Elisha, an Old Testament prophet, was as bald as a cue ball (2 Kings 2:23).

★ Paul, the guy who wrote half of the New Testament, had some sort of disease that affected his eye sight. He probably carried the name, "the squinting preacher" (Galatians 4:14–15; 2 Corinthians 12:8).

★ As I mentioned in the previous chapter, John Mark chickened out and went home to Mommy on Paul's first missionary journey—but Paul later called him "useful."

There are others, but the point is not many are mentioned. Why? *Because imperfections aren't a big deal!* Your attitude about them, however, is.

If you compare yourself in any way to others, and then get depressed about it, you've fallen right into one of Satan's oldest traps. When he turns your focus inward and gets you thinking only about yourself, you'll have no time or motivation to think of others. That means you won't think about serving them, about loving them, or about caring where they spend their eternity. You'll become selfishly depressed and will either go into hiding, or you'll always seek out others who will build *you* up. It's the old bad self-image trap so many have fallen into. True, if the significant people in your life are always making fun of you, you're likely to feel about an inch high—you may not be able to help having a bad self-image. But most of us blow our imperfections *way* out of proportion. We want to be what Hollywood says is perfect.

I do not recall one person ever mentioning anything about my high-water pants. No one ever played connect the dots on my face, nor did they point and stare or make rude comments. Why? Almost everyone else had zits, too. Losing my hair . . . well . . . my whole youth group made fun of me. But by then I didn't care. In their minds, it helped bring me down to their level. Imperfection loves company.

And that's the point. If you were perfect, no one could relate to you. They'd feel inferior around you. Your life and words would lose their power because people would be too intimidated to watch and listen. Did you know that's why God became one of us? We couldn't relate to Him way off in a heaven we'd never seen. He knew that, so He chose to show us what He was like. True, He lived a perfect life, but through Christ's death on the Cross, He showed us the depth of His love—something we never would have known had He not visited earth 2,000 years ago.

God proves Himself strong in weakness. That's His way. He uses the imperfect to accomplish His plan on earth. The key, then, isn't trying to be perfect; it's being comfortable with who you are—as God made you—and making others comfortable with who *they* are. Yes, some imperfections you can improve on. Go ahead and try if you think you need to, but don't get stuck on it. Let God use you just as you are.

ULTIMATE CHOICE

"Will I realize God created my imperfections for reasons I have perhaps not discovered, or will I try to hide my weaknesses away from others so that my world will never see God's strength?"

BOYS . . .

. . . think imperfections are a sign of weakness, so they never learn to be comfortable with who God made them to be.

MEN . . .

. . . have learned to value their imperfections, knowing that God uses them in order to show Himself strong.

THE WORD

Three different times I begged the Lord to take it [Paul's eye affliction] away. Each time he said, "My gracious favor is all you need. My power works best in your weakness." So now I am glad to boast about my weaknesses, so that the power of Christ may work through me. Since I know it is all for Christ's good, I am quite content with my weaknesses and with insults, hardships, persecutions, and calamities. For when I am weak, then I am strong.

2 CORINTHIANS 12:8–10

Remember, dear brothers and sisters, that few of you were wise in the world's eyes, or powerful, or wealthy when God called you. Instead, God deliberately chose things the world considers foolish in order to shame those who think they are wise. And he chose those who are powerless to shame those who are powerful. God chose things despised by the world, things counted as nothing at all, and used them to bring to nothing what the world considers important, so that no one can every boast in the presence of God.

1 CORINTHIANS 1:26–29

ACTION IDEA

Identify three "imperfections" you think you have. Talk to a parent or youth leader and ask them how *they* think God can use that for His glory.

29 Giving Your Life Away

I wouldn't go so far as to say I'm often *troubled* by the words of Jesus, but sometimes I have to stop, scratch my head, and think. Not everything He said makes sense. This passage from Matthew is a perfect example: "Then Jesus said to the disciples, 'If any of you wants to be my follower, you must put aside your selfish ambition, shoulder your cross, and follow me. If you try to keep your life for yourself, you will lose it. But if you give up your life for me, you will find true life'" (Matthew 16:24–25).

When I read that keeping your life will make you lose it, and giving up your life for Jesus means you'll find true life, I have two reactions: (1) "Huh?" and (2) "I'm certain Jesus knows more than I do, so He is obviously trying to say something important here. What is it?"

Early in my Christian life, I was what could best be described as a *taker.* I took from the Bible as much as I could by reading twenty or thirty chapters a day. I took from other Christians all they knew about Jesus, God, and the faith. I had more questions than a three-year-old at Disneyland. And it wasn't long before I quit skipping by passages I didn't understand and started finding out what they meant. Like this one: "'But among you it should be quite different. Whoever wants to be a leader among you must be your servant, and whoever wants to be first must be the slave of all. For even I, the Son of Man, came here not to be served but to serve others, and to give my life as a ransom for many'" (Mark 10:43–45).

Leadership, Jesus said, meant being a servant. Being first meant being a slave. The Lord came to serve, not to be served. He came to give His life, not try to protect it.

Hmmmmmmm.

Then I ran into this one: "After washing their feet, he put on his robe again and sat down and asked, 'Do you understand what I was doing? You call me "Teacher" and "Lord," and you are right, because it is true. And since I, the Lord and Teacher, have washed your feet, you ought to wash each other's feet. I have given you an example to follow. Do as I have done to you'" (John 13:12–15).

I knew immediately that Jesus wasn't literally talking about washing someone else's feet; He was promoting a deeper value He wanted His followers to own: serving.

"Do as I have done to you."

Are you aware that serving others is exactly the opposite of what our world tells us to do? Growing up, I don't remember my parents ever showing or telling me that serving friends, relatives, and strangers was the way to succeed. My school teachers never said that the way to get the most out of life is to serve. The message I was constantly given, though not in these words, was that "money buys happiness"—that "looking out for number one" should be your main concern.

I began to test God to see if what He was saying in all of these passages was true. If I served others and thought about how to help *them*, I would obtain something I didn't have before. So I began serving. If someone needed a ride, I drove them. If a buddy wanted to borrow five bucks, I loaned it to him. If my church needed someone to set up and take down chairs, I was there for them. If they needed help in the kitchen serving an Easter sunrise breakfast, they could count on me. I looked for ways to serve, God provided them, and I found out Jesus was right. Life was more fun and rewarding than I ever thought possible. Three things happened:

1. I felt like I was doing exactly what Jesus would do. I've grown to learn that it is the nature of God to serve others, not to take from them. He can no more *not* serve than I can stop breathing. He can't help it! Yes, people took advantage of Him, but that didn't stop Him from serving. (And yes, people took advantage of me, too.)

2. I felt like I wasn't actually serving another person, but that I was serving Jesus Christ Himself. Whenever my attitude was such that I wanted to hear "thank-you's" or other words of praise for what I did, I was immediately aware that I was serving for the wrong reasons. But whenever I didn't care who noticed what I did, I knew I was serving God for the right reasons. That made it easier when I felt I was being taken advantage of. Since it was God I was serving anyway, I couldn't *really* be taken advantage of.

3. I knew I was pleasing God. Pleasing God is a tricky thing. I wanted to please Him because it was the right thing to do, but sometimes I felt I had to please Him to keep Him happy; that I somehow had to do things so He'd love me more. It took a while, but I soon learned that serving God to win His favor reduces the Christian faith to a "work." The love of God, as you know, is a gift. It can't be earned.

It's been said that most teenagers think the world revolves around them. To a degree, that can be said about everyone (except maybe Mother Theresa). When you think you're the center of the universe, you're less likely to think about meeting the needs of others.

Here's a tough question: How often do you consciously *think* about serving others? And a tougher one: How often do you *actually serve* someone else—without expecting something in return?

To the degree that you serve others because it's the right thing to do is the degree that you are experiencing what the Christian life is really all about. Serving means allowing Jesus to live and work through you.

Do you think Jesus knew something about experiencing life to the fullest? He was *the* expert. How did He live—and die? He served.

Serving relates perfectly to manhood, because becoming a man means treating others as more important than yourself.

It means having the same mind that Jesus had. It means realizing that you're not the center of the universe.

ULTIMATE CHOICE

"Will I continue to think of myself as the most important person on earth, or will I take on the attitude of Jesus, knowing that the path to true life is found by serving others?"

BOYS . . .

. . . fail to see how essential it is to live a life that counts others as more important.

MEN . . .

. . . know that the path of service isn't an easy—or natural —one to take, but because they have taken on the supernatural life of Jesus, they know it's the right path to take.

THE WORD

"All those who want to be my disciples must come and follow me, because my servants must be where I am. And if they follow me, the Father will honor them."

JOHN 12:26

ACTION IDEA

This week, try to think of one way to serve these people:

★ each family member

★ a friend

★ a stranger

30 *Who Do You Say Jesus Is?*

Of all of the daily decisions you'll have to make in life, none is more important than, "What should I do with Jesus today?" Your answer to that question will hinge upon *who you actually think Jesus is.*

If you've ever read through Matthew, by the time you get to chapter 16, the disciples had been with Jesus a couple of years. They had observed Him in dozens of different situations. He'd performed miracles and taught like no one had ever before. Having recently spent several intense days with thousands of people, they were finally alone. It was here that Jesus asked them a question—a question designed to find the answer to another, much more important question.

> *"Who do people say that the Son of Man is?"*
> *"Well," they replied, "some say John the Baptist, some say Elijah, and others say Jeremiah or one of the other prophets."*
> *Then he asked them, "Who do you say I am?"*
> *Simon Peter answered, "You are the Messiah, the Son of the living God."*
> MATTHEW 16:13–16

Jesus wanted to hear from their own mouths who *they* thought He was. We're not told how much time they spent thinking about that question, and we don't know if they took a vote and asked Peter to give their collective answer. All we're told is what Peter said. For once in his life, he came through with the right answer!

Now, Jesus asks *you:* "Who do your friends say that I am?"

If He asked you that question, you'd probably answer, "A good teacher, a myth, a Jewish carpenter, some sort of prophet." Your *Christian* friends would perhaps say, "Savior." "The Lord."

Then He'd follow it up with the question He's most concerned with: "Who do *you* say that I am?"

Be careful now. What you would *say* at this point doesn't mean much. I'm not there to listen and your youth leader can't hear, either. It's just you and God. You don't have to impress anyone, and heaven is not a breath away.

The apostle Paul said that confessing Jesus with our mouths is important (see Romans 10:9), but what's just as important is what you truly believe—on the inside. This inside choice—a daily choice—is what will determine how quickly and how strongly your acquisition of manhood actually occurs. You see, there are many young boys who know *about* Jesus, but by their actions and speech, they prove they do not actually *know* Jesus—at least not too well.

Did you notice that Jesus didn't ask His disciples what the people thought about His teachings? He didn't want comments on how well He could make bread appear out of nowhere. He didn't need praise for opening the eyes of the blind. He didn't even want them to point out His obvious perfection. He wanted a heart-to-heart reaction on *who He was.*

There's a good chance you've given Jesus an initial reaction to who He is. At your baptism, a camp, or to your parents, you've perhaps asserted that Jesus Christ is your savior; that you want *Him* to pay the penalty for your sin instead of yourself. But is that confession a one-time vote of confidence or a daily choice? For salvation, as I hope you know, one time from the heart can get you covered for eternity. For Christian maturation and Christian manhood, however, waking up each day and from your heart asking Jesus Christ to be your Lord, ruler, and best friend is how you get it done. But you won't do that if your picture of Jesus is wrong or out of focus. Jesus isn't an adversary, a myth, your parent's God of choice, or the way your youth leader keeps his job. You must *own* Him for yourself. He must be *your* Lord, *your* best friend, *your* savior, *your* confidant, *your* God.

Is He?

To become the man that God wants you to be—especially in this world where daily distractions tend to crowd Jesus out of the picture—daily proclamations to Jesus about what you want His role to be in your life are the only way to make it.

ULTIMATE CHOICE

"Will I make the wise choice, allowing Jesus to be all He wants to be each day, or will I forget?"

BOYS . . .

. . . delay choosing Jesus for as long as they can in order to stay in control of their own lives.

MEN . . .

. . . know that this daily choice is the most important one they can make, and they choose wisely.

THE WORD

When Jesus heard what had happened, he found the man [whom Jesus healed from his blindness] and said, "Do you believe in the Son of Man?"

The man answered, "Who is he, sir, because I would like to."

"You have seen him," Jesus said, "and he is speaking to you!"

"Yes, Lord," the man said, "I believe!" And he worshipped Jesus.

JOHN 9:35–38

ACTION IDEA

Think about what it would take to help you remember to *daily* make Jesus Christ your number-one priority each new day. Then make a commitment to *doing* those things.

31 *True Courage*

For twenty-five points each, identify the biblical hero:

1. This man was told not to pray to his unseen God, and if he did, the consequences would certainly come back to bite him. Who was he?

2. This man was told to go to a city and tell them to repent. At first he ran away, but soon he learned the value of swallowing God's commands instead of getting swallowed himself. Who was he?

3. This man once swore he never even knew a man he'd spent three years with. But one event in history made the whole world see what he was really made of. Who was the man? For an extra ten points, what was the event?

4. This prophet confronted a king with the truth, not knowing if when the king understood the riddle, who would be brought low. Who was he?

5. This man once put to death anyone who followed Jesus, but soon he was willing to risk his own life dozens of times simply for the chance to tell another soul about the One who was alive. Who was he?

6. This man chose to run from the advances of a queen instead of dishonor his earthly and heavenly king. Who was he?

Out of a possible 160 points, how did you do? The answers are at the bottom of page 124. If you earned more than 125 points, then you know something of courage.

The point of this little quiz is to illustrate that the Bible is packed full of courageous acts done by courageous men. I could have talked also about Moses, Joshua, Noah, Abraham, David, Josiah, Nehemiah, Gideon, Samson, Samuel, Barnabas, James, John, and many others. It's easy to conclude that God put more stories about courage in the Bible than anything else. He must hold courage in high regard.

Are you courageous? Do you even know what it means?

Courage is doing what is right in the face of consequences, large or small. It's closely tied to several other values God holds high: honor, integrity, perseverance. It's not caving in when the pressure is on.

Most courageous acts in the Bible occurred in a split-second decision. The same can be said for those modern-day people of courage who have fought in wars, served as peace officers, or rescued a child from a burning house. They were at the right place at the right time, and made the right decision.

But is it luck? Do people who perform courageous acts ever ponder the choice they need to make, then, after weighing all of costs and benefits, intellectually choose the right thing to do?

Most courageous deeds are done by people who don't have time to think about it. Because their character is strong, however, they simply do what comes naturally. They are people who automatically respond courageously, not because they want to be heroes, but because they hold strong internal values that are more important than life itself. Look at the six I mentioned at the beginning, and you can spot their values almost immediately:

★ Daniel could not allow himself to worship any other God. He wouldn't even fake it to save his skin.

★ When Jonah came to his senses (oftentimes, God gives us a second chance to make a right decision), he told an entire city to repent or prepare to become crispy critters.

★ Peter knew Jesus had risen from the dead, and he knew he had been forgiven by Him. His love for Jesus was so strong, he had to tell others.

★ Nathan stood on the truth, so he had to be honest with King David about his adulterous and murderous decisions—no matter what it could have cost him.

★ Paul, like Peter, had personally experienced the resurrection of Jesus. And because he had been forgiven much, he loved much, and risked his life countless times just for the chance to tell the world about his wonderful Savior.

★ Joseph immediately said no to a sexually-charged opportunity that many men would have said yes to without a second thought. Moral purity was a value deeply imbedded in his heart.

Modern-day heroes, if they don't hold human life in high regard, won't risk their own life, won't stand up for the unborn, and they likely won't take good care of the life God gave them.

If you are perceptive, you can see that courage is born of conviction. Convictions are deep-seeded beliefs that guide everyday decisions.

What are *your* convictions?

★ Is Jesus Christ alive and living in your heart, or is He just another man the adults in your life *say* is alive to try to keep you in line?

★ Do you believe there are moral absolutes like honesty, sexual purity, and being fair with *everyone*, or can you bend any situation that arises to meet your own selfish ends?

The simple truth is: If you have the right convictions, you're the type who will one day do something courageous. If you don't, you won't.

ULTIMATE CHOICE

"Will I be a man of conviction so I will be ready to do something courageous should God so lead, or will I continually change what I believe based on the moment?"

BOYS . . .

. . . avoid having convictions so as to never face the physical or social "danger" that could result by having them.

MEN . . .

. . . live each day with strong, biblical convictions that guide their every decision.

THE WORD

"These things I have spoken to you, that in Me you may have peace. In the world you have tribulation, but take courage; I have overcome the world."

JOHN 16:33, NASB

"But you, be strong and do not lose courage, for there is reward for your work."

2 CHRONICLES 15:7, NASB

ACTION IDEA

Write down five convictions you currently have and ask yourself this question about each: Is this a conviction that could one day make a difference to someone besides myself?

Answers:
1. Daniel; 2. Jonah; 3. Peter (Acts 3–4), the resurrection of Jesus;
4. Nathan (2 Samuel 12); 5. Paul (Acts 9 and 2 Corinthians 11);
6. Joseph (Genesis 39)

32

Hearing Your Father's Voice

Seeing a lifeless body is something a kid never forgets. I know I won't.

It was 7 A.M. and my dad and I were beachcombing in a misty fog near Yachats on the Oregon Coast. My goal was to discover everything a ten-year-old boy knows is cool: starfish to throw like Frisbees, sea anemones to poke with a stick, intact clam shells, whole sand dollars, perhaps even a live crab walking sideways toward the ocean (then, of course, I'd try to pick it up without getting pinched). The tide that day was way out. It seemed like a mile between where I'd dug tunnels the day before in front of a pounding surf and where we were walking. Dad held the plastic bag to place all of my newfound treasures in.

Then high up on the beach I saw something green. *A patch of seaweed washed up on the beach,* I thought.

"Dad, I'm going to run up to that clump of seaweed. I bet there's a live crab trying to get out."

"See that seagull picking at it, Son?" he said. "You might be right. I'll keep moving to see what's ahead so we don't miss anything."

I took off at a sprint for about sixty yards. As I approached the green blob, I slowed down and looked closely.

"*Dad!*" I yelled. "It's a man! Dad, it's a man!"

"What?"

"A man! It's a man!"

He walked up slowly and deliberately, the bag of shells swinging from side to side. Though I tried to coax him to hurry, his pace never changed. About twenty feet from the man, he took a long look and said a few simple words that I'd heard him say a million times before.

"Well I'll be darned."

As we stared at what was left of the lifeless body (and feetless and armless and headless), he said it again.

"Well I'll be darned. You're right."

Though he told me not to look, my virgin eyes had already been initiated. The green color I'd noticed came from his dark green pants. The seagull had been picking at what was left of his body. We found out later he'd been in the water for six weeks! *The Oregonian* reported that "tourists had discovered the body of Arthur Jensen, 33, a fisherman." Needless to say, I was the hit at show-and-tell my first day of school two weeks later. And the picture of that day—including my dad's reaction—will stay with me forever.

Whenever something happened that amazed my dad, he always said the same thing. "Well I'll be darned." I remember a *few* other things he told me in life, but actually, not much. As I've mentioned, my parents were soon to be divorced. My contact with him until he passed away years ago was minimal (as many father/son relationships go). Yes, he took me fishing, came to a lot of my games, was there for graduation, my wedding, and holidays. He called. I called. I loved him very much, but there are so many things I wished I could have heard him say.

To my recollection he didn't sing me songs or read me stories when I was little. I don't think he ever prayed for me (since we weren't a Christian family). He never told me about how Jesus died to save me from the penalty of my sin. I didn't hear, "I love you, Son, but God loves you even more." He never challenged me to save myself for marriage (in fact, just the opposite).

My father was a nice guy most of the time, a hard worker, but now that he's gone, I can't hear his voice today. The reason, I suppose, is he never told me anything eternal or long lasting —at least not anything that comes to mind beyond, "Well I'll be darned."

Unfortunately, like me, not every guy has a dad around who takes the initiative to talk about the unseen God who is there. Hopefully, you're one of the lucky ones who has heard your dad talk about what makes a "man of God," that "a man keeps his promises," "a man treats women with respect," "a man has the courage to stand firm when others want to take him the wrong direction," and "a Christian man doesn't just know *about* Jesus Christ, he *knows* Him."

These are the type of words between a father and son that sink in—that make a difference. Of course, those words have to be backed up with actions, and often they are. If you have that type of dad, a Christian father in word and deed, be sure to tell him *and* God "thanks" once in a while. You're one of the few.

I didn't, but when I became a Christian just out of high school, God provided the perfect source to hear things that mattered: His Word. Actually, it's the source *every* guy can look to each day. It's amazing how the heavenly Father's words can stick in your brain. The reason is because it's *supernatural,* eternal, true. When someone hears real truth over and over—God's truth—it sticks. It makes a difference.

Are you giving attention to God's Word?

I don't want to encourage you into a faith based on how well you perform for God. That is, God's not going to love you any more if you read your Bible once a week—or seven times a week. Many years ago, I went fourteen straight months reading my Bible without missing a day. I intentionally ended my streak because the streak had become more important than my relationship with God. But what I learned during those fourteen months was that my love for God had grown. I'd given Him a chance to make Himself real to me, and He delivered. His Word *was* truth! And it kept reverberating through my head right when I needed it. I made better choices, I responded the way Jesus would, and I learned what it meant to walk with God. All because I made the conscious choice to open the Book and let God talk to me.

You may not appreciate the truth of God's Word right now. Perhaps it seems too intimidating to pick up (except when you go to church). But one day when you find yourself in need of knowing what the right thing to do is, I hope you're able to realize exactly what your Father in heaven would say. He isn't silent. He is ready to speak to you in a loud and clear voice. I hope you're a man who's ready to listen.

ULTIMATE CHOICE

"Will I choose to hear God's voice through His Word, giving Him the attention He deserves, or will I trust other voices whose words are not eternal—whose counsel does not always come straight from heaven?"

BOYS . . .

. . . make the easy choice to keep the Book on the shelf, believing they have their whole life to hear from God.

MEN . . .

. . . make the disciplined choice to give attention to God's Word by making the Bible part of their lives on a consistent basis, not because they have to win God's favor, but because they want to hear God's voice throughout their lives.

THE WORD

"Here I am! I stand at the door and knock. If anyone hears my voice and opens the door, I will come in and eat with him, and he with me."

REVELATION 3:20, NIV

But Jesus told him, "No! The Scriptures say, 'People need more than bread for their life; they must feed on every word of God.'"

MATTHEW 4:4

ACTION IDEA

To begin the lifetime habit of hearing from God by reading your Bible, think of two things you do every day. Perhaps it's a shower and breakfast, or washing your face and making your bed. Allow some time in between those two things to begin learning the joy of having God talk directly to you.

33

You Can Do Anything!

I've told a lot of personal stories in these pages, but I want to give you an even clearer picture of who I was. Not to brag or make you feel sorry for me, but to show you what the title of this chapter suggests.

Besides having very little spiritual influence, everything seemed great in life until my dad left to "find himself." He divorced a devoted wife of seventeen years, my brother, sister, and me—twelve-year-old Greg. We moved from the big house where all of my good family memories come from to a three-bedroom, ant-infested duplex. The little critters were so bad in this dump, I remember several nights where I'd be up at two in the morning vacuuming them from every corner of room until I knew they were all gone. A couple of years later, Mom married a three-time loser and wife beater. That marriage lasted three months. We moved again, this time into an apartment. There weren't as many ants, but the ones we did have were big carpenter ants. You know, the kind that carry hammers.

Survival for me meant participating in sports, playing poker with buddies, and eventually becoming a closet stoner. (Since I was an athlete, I couldn't flaunt my drugs.) Mom remarried a third time and moved away. I moved in with my dad—who was on *his* third marriage. He was a "nice" alcoholic (interpretation: not abusive), a professional gambler, caring, but still pretty mixed up. We smoked dope several times *together* during my senior year of high school (which was really weird, even though all of my friends thought it was cool).

129

I took an aptitude test early that year, and the printout said that with my skills and desires, I would be perfect for floor covering/textile industry (I'm not making this up). I decided instead to follow my brother's footsteps and go into the Navy. My high school GPA was 3.00—thanks to those two P.E. classes per term I did not read an entire book from junior high through high school. I took the SAT tests (just in case) and scored a 760—that was my total (1600 is perfect).

As you can tell, my future wasn't too promising. A few months before graduation, a college that must have been exceedingly desperate sent me a letter saying they'd like me to come to their school to play basketball. Since this turned out to be the only college that would accept me (because of my stunning SAT scores), I went.

It was at this point in my life that God finally got my attention. Through the influence of my girlfriend, who was a Christian, I allowed Jesus to take control. I could see that *my* efforts weren't going to lead me anywhere, so what did I have to lose?

The short story on the years since then is this: I graduated from a Christian college with two degrees (Biblical Studies and Psychology) and a 3.5 GPA. I went directly from college into full-time ministry with a youth organization called Campus Life/Youth for Christ. For ten years I was able to lead hundreds of teens toward a faith in Jesus Christ. I counseled students, families, and college students trying to find their way. Add in a wife (my high school sweetheart) and two boys, and life was more wonderful than I could ever imagine. For five years I was the editor of *Breakaway*, Focus on the Family's magazine for teen boys (which you ought to be getting if you're not). Each month I was able to point 100,000 boys to the Savior. Along the way, I've written more than one hundred magazine articles and twenty books (this from a guy who didn't even read one until age eighteen!).

What God has done with my life since I allowed Him to run it I simply cannot believe. All of my "thank-you's" don't seem enough. I vividly remember my life before I came to know Him, how dead-end it was. When I told God I wanted to reach teens that were as messed up as I was, I had no idea He would come through beyond my wildest imagination. But that's the way He works. His Word is true when it says, "Now glory be to God! By his mighty power at work within us, he is able to accomplish infinitely more than we would ever dare to ask or hope" (Ephesians 3:20).

I could point to a hundred other lives and tell dozens of stories that would amplify and prove this verse to be true. But the one story I can point to with absolute confidence about God's ability to take a life and make something of it is my own. I know for a fact that with Jesus Christ on the throne of your life (that means He's king), you can do *anything*.

What are your dreams? How big can you think?

Do not *ever* limit God on what you think He can do through you. As long as you keep your life focused in His direction (the only "catch" to the deal), He will fulfill the promises in His Word. He *will* give you infinitely more than you would ever dare ask or hope.

ULTIMATE CHOICE

"Will I try to achieve my own dreams by my own effort, or will I allow God to take control of my life so that I can achieve the dreams He gives me?"

BOYS . . .

. . . have a hard time understanding the fact that God wants to make their life better than they ever thought imaginable.

MEN . . .

. . . know that anything is possible with God, and they allow Him do all that He wants to do with their life.

THE WORD

Take delight in the LORD, and he will give you your heart's desires. Commit everything you do to the LORD. Trust him, and he will help you.

PSALM 37:4–5

The LORD is righteous in everything he does; he is filled with kindness. The LORD is close to all who call on him, yes, to all who call on him sincerely. He fulfills the desires of those who fear him; he hears their cries for help and rescues them. The LORD protects all those who love him, but he destroys the wicked.

PSALM 145:17–20

ACTION IDEA

Come to the conclusion in your own mind that God wants to rule your life, not to make it worse, but to make it better beyond your wildest dreams. Think about the things in your life that might get in God's way of achieving His best for you—then make a choice to do something about them.

34

Life Is a Classroom

lot of males are dumb jocks. Life to them *is* a sport. They drink it up. End of commercial. Far too many are "head turners." We discussed this earlier, but basically their goal is to not miss staring at any female in tight clothes or a skirt. Since a dog sniffs everywhere—and *they're* considered normal—a man can look at anything and be normal, too. (Comparing that type of male to a dog comes easily.) Many others are simply couch potato idiots. Fun begins and ends with the TV remote, a bag of chips, and a cold one.

The comparisons are endless, but my goal isn't to put every guy down like a card-carrying feminist (since all three of these comparisons have described me at one time in my life); it's to make a simple point: few of us males are learners, readers, or "noticers." Getting wisdom from a variety of sources isn't a goal.

Since you're reading this book, you may be a reader. Good work. But are you a learner or a noticer?

At this point, I can hear the collective thoughts of thousands of guys reading these words thinking, *Why would I want to be one of those?* To which I'll respond, "Great question? You're close to being a noticer!"

Unfortunately, many teachers and classes have trained us guys to have a distaste for books, reading, and learning. How is it done? When I was in junior high, my P.E. teacher always made us run when he wanted to punish us. I can still hear him saying, "Around the tree!" "Four laps around the track!"

"Twenty laps around the gym . . . and no cutting corners!" Years later, I still hate to run. No, I *HATE* to run!

That's the way it can be with books. All books seem to do is prevent you from watching TV, spending time with the guys, listening to music, and doing other stuff you like to do. Since most of us males are the active types, we'd rather be *doing* than reading. Plus, no one applauds for us after we read a book like they do after we hit a three-pointer. Not all males have to perform athletically, true, but a high percentage don't do much unless it has some sort of immediate reward. Sadly, that attitude about reading and learning carries over into adulthood. The result is we have millions of guys who are proud of the fact they haven't read a book since high school.

A boy tracking his progress toward Christian manhood must pay attention to what he's paying attention to.

Jesus made a clear statement to His twelve disciples, when, after feeding four thousand people, He started talking about the "yeast" of the Pharisees and Herod. He was making the point that the words of these Jewish leaders, though sprinkled lightly through the crowds like yeast, would soon have an encompassing effect on the masses—perhaps even *them*.

What did the disciples think about that statement? Get this, "They decided he was saying this because they hadn't brought any bread" (Mark 8:16). It wasn't just one or two numbskull disciples who concluded Jesus was worried about having bread (after He had just fed four thousand people!); they *all* came to that conclusion! If they hadn't been such complete idiots, it would have been comical.

John: "What was Jesus talking about, 'yeast of Herod'?"

James: "Not just yeast of Herod, but of the Pharisees, too, you little knucklehead. Are you deaf or something?"

John: "Who you calling a knucklehead, lamebrain?"

Peter: "Cut it out you two. You'd think after all this time hearing Jesus talk about brotherly love, you two brothers would finally quit eating at each other. By the way, who brought lunch?"

Thomas: "Lunch? I doubt it's lunchtime already."

Matthew: "That reminds me, I'm hungry."

Andrew: "Jesus must be hungry, too. Judas, you were in charge of buying food. Where is it?"

Judas: "Huh?"

Peter: "Oh man, Jesus is going to be mad at us now. Not only don't we have lunch, there's not even any hunks of moldy bread to get Jesus started."

Finally, Jesus breaks into the conversation (no doubt after having a good laugh).

> "Why are you so worried about having no food? Won't you ever learn or understand? Are your hearts too hard to take it in? 'You have eyes—can't you see? You have ears—can't you hear?' Don't you remember anything at all? What about the five thousand men I fed with five loaves of bread? How many baskets of leftovers did you pick up afterward?"
>
> "Twelve," they said.
>
> "And when I fed the four thousand with seven loaves, how many large baskets of leftovers did you pick up?"
>
> "Seven," they said.
>
> "Don't you understand even yet?" he asked them. (Mark 8:17–21)

After turning away and looking toward the heavens (possibly praying that His Father would send Him twelve other guys), Jesus stops and faces His twelve followers, hearing them all say in unison, "Oh, yeah, now we get it! How could we have been so stupid? Yeast of the Pharisees, right." When He turns to keep walking, all of the disciples are looking at each other, scratching their heads and shrugging their shoulders. I can see Jesus with a big grin on His face. He knows they still don't get it.

They were ignorant fisherman only worried about who brought lunch. (And who they should blame for *not* bringing it.) They couldn't grasp that Jesus was telling them to watch out for teaching that could destroy them. "Notice what's going on around you," Jesus was saying.

And He's saying it to you today.

* "Watch people and learn."

* "Perceive what lessons you can grasp from others so you don't make their mistakes."

* "Read all that you can get your hands on. Gain knowledge about life, the world, and yourself. Don't settle for being a dumb jock, only worried about where your next pizza is coming from!"

* "Notice what's going on in your world so you'll know how to correctly respond to it; so you'll know what is trying to steal your joy and rob you of what I want to give."

* "Have eyes that see and ears that hear."

If you want to be known as a wise guy, hear what David has to say. "Teach the wise, and they will be wiser. Teach the righteous, and they will learn more" (Proverbs 9:9).

Jesus said it, David said it, and I have reminded you they said it. Got it yet?

ULTIMATE CHOICE

"Will I choose to ignore the fact that all of life is a classroom, or will I see with my eyes and perceive with my heart all that God is trying to teach me as I walk closely with Him?"

BOYS . . .

. . . do not see the value in learning all they can about themselves and life.

MEN . . .

. . . know there is much to learn by reading, by listening, and by noticing what is going on in their world. All help them be a better man, better Christian, and better husband and father.

THE WORD

Wise people treasure knowledge, but the babbling of a fool invites trouble.

PROVERBS 10:14

Let those who are wise listen to these proverbs and become even wiser. And let those who understand receive guidance by exploring the depth of meaning in these proverbs, parables, wise sayings, and riddles.

PROVERBS 1:5–6

ACTION IDEA

For a week, practice asking yourself this question after each significant experience, each news show, every TV show, each encounter with other people: "What can I learn from this?"

35

Going For It!

Have you ever snow skied before? If you have, you'll quickly notice there are three types of skiers.

1. The beginning skier. This guy shows up at the slopes in jeans, cloth gloves, no stocking cap, and rented skis—140's. He thinks snowplowing is what is going on in the parking lot and the black diamond is a new rare gem discovery. But he doesn't care. He came because his friend told him how much fun—and how easy it was, and he's going to show him he can do it. Spurning all advice, his first two hours are spent in total frustration. He's falling off of the lift, falling down the hill, getting soaked to the skin, becoming half-frostbitten—he's miserable. Before noon, he heads to the lodge and vows to one day get that "friend" who invited him to the mountain.

After lunch and four hot chocolates, he caves in to the peer pressure of his friends. What he has vowed never to do again, he does. He gives it another try. This time he's a bit more motivated to learn. He listens when someone tells him how to get on and off of the ski lift. His feet finally clue in that they must point inward if he wants to slow down or stop. Turning somehow becomes easier. He's getting the hang of it! And he even starts talking ski language. "Hey, did you see me do a daffy off of that six-foot mogul on the blue run by the green chair?" He's not ready to go down the face of the most treacherous black diamond, but he's learned enough to finally have fun. Sure, his jeans are soaked and his hands are freezing, but being able to stay under control at fifteen miles per hour is a cool feeling. When he scrapes up enough dough again, he'll be back.

2. The "I'm going to look good in the lodge" skier. This guy comes with all the latest equipment. He's wearing bright yellow one-piece bibs that fit perfectly. Smith goggles, boots, skis and bindings that sell for hundreds. Lift tickets from the past five years are neatly displayed at the end of his jacket zipper. And he's walking around the lodge like he invented skiing, checking out every ski bunny who looks his way. He looks the part, but there's something wrong: He spends little of his time on the slopes! He's at the mountain to look good, be seen, and ski just enough to have a few stories to tell.

3. The "Go For It" skier. This guy has the basic equipment. He's warm, but not color-coordinated. His skis are nice, but they're a bit beat up from overuse. He's the first one up the ski lift, and the fastest going down. He takes fifteen minutes to eat—after the crowds have cleared out. While everyone else has their skis packed in the bus, he's trying to get in one more run. He loves the speed, the snow—and he lives for the challenge of going down a slope that even the ski instructors avoid.

There are also three types of males who are trying to push their way toward Christian manhood.

1. The Beginner. This guy is still growing into his body, has trouble sometimes with his thought life, doesn't understand a lot of the Bible, and is convinced that God loves him, but doesn't know everything there is to know about being a Christian. He tries, gets discouraged, maybe even gets mad at those who try to keep him on the right path. But since he sees others having a good time of it, he decides to keep giving it another try. Soon he's learning the essentials about the faith, knows what to do when he makes a mistake, he's even learned to pray out loud. Becoming a Christian man isn't easy, but it's definitely worth the effort.

2. The "I'm going to look good as a man" male. Or the *"I can look good in church" guy.* This guy believes appearance is everything. He looks the part of a boy growing into a man, but his character and behavior when no one is looking show different. He's learned to play the church game, and perhaps he's even picked up a few secrets about fooling his parents into thinking he's heading the right direction, but inside he wants to stay a boy.

Because he's "successful" at fooling people into thinking he's a Christian man—or heading that direction—he begins to believe that playing the game is how you get by. He unconsciously reasons, *Since everyone is playing it, this is how it's done.*

3. *The "go for it!" guy.* He is single-minded about who he wants to be. He won't settle for staying a beginner, and he knows it's phoney to look good in the lodge. More than anything else, he wants to be a man who is trusted by God and his fellow man to do the right thing. He knows his goal of Christian manhood will have some costs to it, but he's willing to pay them. Why? It's the right thing to do. And he doesn't do the right thing to impress his parents; he does it because men do the right thing.

☆ ☆ ☆

If you've made it all the way through this book, you've been challenged in areas you probably didn't even know existed. Along with being motivated to pursue Christian manhood, you've probably wondered if it's even attainable. You perhaps think yourself so far away from these ideals that it may not be worth the effort. If that's where your brain is taking you, you'll be a beginner who gives up, you'll occasionally look good at church, but you'll never be a "go for it" type of Christian man.

Is that what you really want?

I'll spare you the football coach challenges to your masculinity if you're bending toward heading away from Christian manhood. But this I can promise: I have met dozens of males who "never raised the bar" for their lives. Instead of trying for something just beyond their reach, they've settled. Eventually, each of these men who settle live to regret they didn't push themselves to greater levels of masculine maturity. They look the part of a man, occasionally acted the part, but Christian manhood was never their focus. They now must live with their regrets.

I've never met a man who, with Jesus Christ in his heart and the goal of becoming a man just like his Savior, regrets the challenge. While it's a never-ending process, at some points filled with mistakes, that goal of Christian manhood always proves itself to be a target worth shooting for.

I hope and pray that you're becoming a man who will throughout his life shoot for the target God wants you to hit.

ULTIMATE CHOICE

"Will I give up, settle for looking good, or move up the ladder to become a man, keeping Christian manhood in my sights as the goal?"

BOYS . . .

. . . try to stay boys as long as they can. Some never do become men, even when their body says they're adults.

MEN . . .

. . . realize that in some areas they can at least stay young, but in areas of character, they must become like Jesus—the ultimate example of a godly man.

THE WORD

Your attitude should be the same that Christ Jesus had. Though he was God, he did not demand and cling to his rights as God. He made himself nothing; he took the humble position of a slave and appeared in human form. And in human form he obediently humbled himself even further by dying a criminal's death on a cross. Because of this, God raised him up to the heights of heaven and gave him a name that is above every other name.

PHILIPPIANS 2:5–9

ACTION IDEA

Over the next few weeks, begin to decide what type of male you want to be—a boy who looks like a man, or a boy who's taken the challenge to become the Christian man God wants him to be.

One Last Word

If

If you can keep your head when all about you
Are losing theirs and blaming it on you;
If you can trust yourself when all men doubt you,
But make allowance for their doubting too;
If you can wait and not be tired by waiting,
Or, being lied about, don't deal in lies,
Or, being hated, don't give way to hating,
And yet don't look too good, nor talk too wise;
If you can dream—and not make dreams your master;
If you can think—and not make thoughts your aim;
If you can meet with triumph and disaster
And treat those two impostors just the same;
If you can bear to hear the truth you've spoken
Twisted by knaves to make a trap for fools,
Or watch the things you gave your life to broken,
And stoop and build 'em up with worn out tools;
If you can make one heap of all your winnings
And risk it on one turn of pitch-and-toss,
And lose, and start again at your beginnings
And never breathe a word about your loss;
If you can force your heart and nerve and sinew
To serve your turn long after they are gone,
And so hold on when there is nothing in you
Except the will which says to them: "Hold on";
If you can talk with crowds and keep your virtue,
Or walk with kings—nor lose the common touch;
If neither foes nor loving friends can hurt you;
If all men count with you, but none too much;
If you can fill the unforgiving minute
With sixty seconds' worth of distance run
Yours is the Earth and everything that's in it,
And—which is more—you'll be a Man, my son!
—RUDYARD KIPLING

142

Group Discussion Questions

★ What are some of the "pictures" your friends at school have of Jesus? Where did they get those impressions?

★ Did you ever have the wrong picture of Jesus? How did it get cleared up?

★ How can you discern where to find the right picture of Jesus when so many things that bear the tag "religious" don't represent Him well?

★ What is it about the life of Christ that proves He's the real deal?

★ What does the word "competition" mean to you?

★ How has TV sports influenced you in your attitudes about winning and losing?

★ Do you agree with the point that simply competing is winning?

★ Have you ever felt like a loser if you've lost? If so, was that the right way to feel?

★ What can competition teach you about succeeding as a Christian?

CHAPTER 3

★ Describe your relationship with your dad right now? Are you happy with it?

★ What does your father do to show you his love? What do you do to show love to him?

143

★ In what ways have you accomplished or attempted the "tips" mentioned in the chapter?

★ What are a few things you're learning from your dad while watching his life? (good and bad)

★ Name one thing about your dad's character that you want for yourself.

★ Is it a goal of yours to become best friends with your dad? Why, or why not?

CHAPTER 4

★ In what ways have you been a couch potato Christian?

★ What spiritual vitamins are you taking that are adding to your growth as a believer? Do you think that any are unknowingly keeping you from putting on spiritual muscle?

★ Talk about your Bible study habits with the Bible? Are you satisfied with the attention you give it?

★ What are some obstacles that are keeping you from putting more time into reading and understanding God's Word? How can they be overcome?

CHAPTER 5

★ In what areas do you feel the most pressure from friends? How about from others?

★ Is this pressure intentional, or does it happen without anyone recognizing it?

★ Why do you think peer pressure affects teenagers so much?

★ What does it show about your character if you're always caving into the pressure?

★ Becoming comfortable with your own set of values is your key to withstanding the pressure. What will it take for you to come to that point where you're feeling good about who you are?

Chapter 6

★ What has your family consciously taught you about people of different races? How about unconsciously?

★ Why do you think race differences are such a big deal in our culture?

★ What can you realistically do to keep yourself "color-blind"?

★ When you see injustice between people, race motivated or not, what do you think your response should be?

★ Talk about the points made about how to overcome the color barrier in your friendships. How possible is that for you to do?

Chapter 7

★ What are the "good pride" things in your life that you're proud of?

★ When does your "bad pride" have a tendency to take over? (Talk about specific instances.)

★ Do you feel pride is a problem with you, or can you occasionally take the high road and be humble?

★ Why do you think God is so against the pride of man?

★ Is your pride keeping you from having a clean relationship with anyone right now?

Chapter 8

★ Share your answers to the "finish the sentence" at the beginning of the chapter.

★ What "brush strokes" have the most weight in your life on how you feel about yourself?

★ Why is knowing the truth about yourself from God's perspective more important than listening to others?

★ How can you begin to internalize that truth on a daily basis?

★ How can you filter out the lies you hear about yourself so you're not affected by their power?

CHAPTER 9

* Tell the truth: Are you using your mouth as a weapon to make you look better in front of others?

* Talk about a few guys at school who are good at this. Why do you think they put others down so often?

* Have you seen the destructive consequences your words can have on others?

* What will it take to clean up your words so you don't destroy your neighbors?

CHAPTER 10

* Talk about the limits your parents have put on your media diet. Do you think they're fair? What would you do differently?

* Do you know any guys at school who are so influenced by what they watch, that you wonder how they're going to turn out?

* Has your mind been polluted in any way (now that you're thinking about it)?

* What are the best ways to discern good from evil when it comes to knowing what to set your eyes on?

CHAPTER 11

* Do you ever wonder why you were created? What answers have you come up with so far?

* What natural talents do you have? How about special gifts?

* Have you ever thought God gave you these talents and gifts to serve others instead of serve yourself?

* How can your gifts allow you to serve others?

* Do you think God can (or will) take away what He's given you if you don't use them for others?

CHAPTER 12

★ Share your answers to what you were afraid of when you were younger.

★ What are you most afraid of now?

★ Have you ever tried to overcome a fear? What, and how, did you do?

★ In what ways, if any, do you fear the crowd?

★ How can God help you overcome the fears you have?

CHAPTER 13

★ What promises do you want your dad to always keep?

★ What promises do you think you should always keep?

★ Why is keeping promises so important?

★ When are you most tempted to break promises you've made to yourself? to God? to your parents?

CHAPTER 14

★ In what ways do you feel you honor your mother? your father?

★ In what ways have you dishonored them?

★ If you didn't honor your parents, could you ever hope to honor God?

★ How are things going in your home as you're getting closer to leaving the nest? What causes conflict? What doesn't?

★ What would it take for you to honor your parents even more?

CHAPTER 15

★ Would it be too weird to go to someone who has something against you and get it right? Why?

★ Why are clean relationships the ultimate to God?

★ How will your mind have to change for relationships to become the ultimate for you?

CHAPTER 16

★ On a scale of 1 to 10 (1 being weak, 10 being strong), how would you rate your conscience? Why?

★ How does your conscience properly develop?

★ Can your conscience get "overly" developed? How?

★ Why do you need a conscience?

★ What are the percentages for what keeps you in line: parents: _____ others: _____ yourself: _____?

★ How good are you at confessing your sin to God? Do you recognize the wall is torn down between you two every time you do confess?

CHAPTER 17

★ Have you ever had a friend start drifting off into the deep end? What did you do, if anything?

★ Would you want a friend to talk to you if you began to unknowingly head toward trouble? Would you listen?

★ Would the points mentioned as to what you can do to confront a friend work for you?

★ What would Jesus do if He were in your shoes?

CHAPTER 18

★ What are the toughest decisions you'll be making in the years ahead?

★ Who will you listen to for the right advice?

★ How do you feel about going to others for advice?

★ Has God ever used someone else and his or her advice to point you the right direction?

CHAPTER 19

★ How do some guys treat females at school?

★ If a girl were to describe how you treat her, what would she say? (If you said, "It depends on who it is," re-read the chapter.)

★ Why do some girls get treated poorly?

★ Have you ever tried to defend some girl from an ignorant guy? What was the result? Why don't you do it more often?

★ Are there ways you can start treating your mother better?

CHAPTER 20

★ Talk about your attitudes on church through the years.

★ Describe your "perfect" church.

★ What could you do to start serving more at church?

★ Which of the six points mentioned in the chapter apply to you most?

★ In the "Action Idea" section, read the passages together and discuss.

CHAPTER 21

★ When have you most been tempted to cheat? How often do you succumb to that temptation?

★ When your school days are done, do you think a habit of cheating will have any affect on the rest of your life?

★ What do your parents want most: good grades no matter what, or no cheating and hard work (and let the grades fall where they may)?

★ What are the best ways to break a cheating habit?

CHAPTER 22

★ Talk about some of the tragic circumstances you are personally aware of. Does it make you ask the "why?" question?

★ Are you the type who needs to know the why to everything, or is it easy to trust God in the unanswered questions?

★ Answer these questions that appear in the chapter: If something bad happened to you today, what would you do? What will you think? Does God get the blame?

Or will you turn to Him like a trusted friend? Will Christ's death on the cross have any meaning for you, or will you shake your fist in the air and tell Him He isn't worthy of your love and obedience? Will you be tempted to think He doesn't even exist?

CHAPTER 23

★ When you think of the word "contentment," what comes to your mind?

★ Is it tough to stay contented in any of these areas: possessions; social status; appearance; applause from the crowd?

★ Do you ever have the fear that you won't measure up to the expectations of others?

★ How strong is your confidence that God is with you now, and will always be right next to your side?

★ Is pleasing God more important than pleasing the crowd?

CHAPTER 24

★ If you were to rate your father from one to ten on the anger meter (ten being an ultra-hothead), where would he be?

★ Where do you rate?

★ What makes your cork pop most of all?

★ Have you ever made any attempt to keep your anger under control? How have you done?

★ Are you the type that needs the "control" in order to feel right?

★ How can you best learn to "give up" so that allowing God to stay in control is more important to you?

★ How can you move the character quality of "self-control" to a higher priority?

CHAPTER 25

★ What temptation causes your head to turn the most: TV/video, magazines, females?

★ Have you tried to stop? What has/hasn't worked?

★ What do you think it means to "take your thoughts captive?"

★ Becoming accountable—being honest with another guy or two about your thought life—is a good potential solution. How do you feel about doing this?

CHAPTER 26

★ Answer the first three questions in the chapter.

★ How do you feel when your parents get on your case for being lazy? Are they right?

★ Why is consistent laziness so destructive?

★ What does it mean to "do your work as unto the Lord"?

★ What will it take to convince you that you can and should do everything to the best of your ability?

CHAPTER 27

★ When you think of the word "leader," what comes to your mind?

★ In what circumstances are you a follower? a leader?

★ Have you ever tried to be a leader and failed or were shot down? How did it make you feel?

★ Do you ever sense God wants you to be more of a leader?

★ What about Mark's life can you relate to most?

★ The leadership suggestions at the end of the chapter . . . which ones could you attempt?

CHAPTER 28

★ Do you have any "imperfections" that you are sensitive about? How sensitive?

★ Have you ever believed that God made a mistake when He created people with "imperfections"? (Or when He created you?)

★ Is it easy or tough to overlook the "imperfections" of others?

★ Do you have a clear picture of yourself as God sees you, or do you tend more to look at yourself the way you think others view you?

★ Whose vote should count more: other people or God? How can God have a stronger voice in your life?

CHAPTER 29

★ Are you convinced that giving your life away means you'll find it?

★ Why do you think serving others is such a big deal to God?

★ How could it become a big deal to you?

★ What are the benefits of giving your life away? The detriments?

CHAPTER 30

★ Who do your friends say that Jesus is?

★ Does their opinion (vocal or silent) about Jesus affect how closely you choose to follow Him?

★ Talk about your own opinions about Jesus. Who do you say He is?

★ Have you ever thought about delaying following Christ until you're out of school so you'll be able to "enjoy yourself" during your teenage years?

★ Why is this not the smart move?

CHAPTER 31

★ Take the courage multiple choice and see how many points you end up with.

★ From your own knowledge of the Bible, who are the most courageous men you admire?

★ Would you say you have the convictions it takes to perform some act of courage? Or are those convictions still developing?

CHAPTER 32

★ What are some things you hear your own father saying, even now? Are they words that make a difference, or are they simple phrases that have no consequence?

★ What can you hear God's voice saying?

★ Is hearing more of God's voice a value for you? Why? Why not?

★ How are you doing at reading your Bible? What could make it better?

CHAPTER 33

★ Talk about people you've known who have been changed by the power of Jesus Christ.

★ Does hearing (or reading) about the story of God's grace in the life of another motivate you in any way to pursue Him more? Why? Why not?

★ What are your dreams for the future? Do you think God wants to take those "dream seedlings" and make them even better?

★ How can God turn your dreams into reality?

CHAPTER 34

★ Would you consider yourself a "noticer"? a learner?

★ Are you at all convinced that being a learner is that important?

★ How do you learn best: reading, listening, watching, or doing?

★ Is obtaining wisdom a high enough value for you to start changing a few of your habits?

CHAPTER 35

★ What type of skier are you? What type of Christian?

★ Have you ever been tempted to simply be the type who "looks good at church"?

★ What will it honestly take before you become a "go for it" type of Christian?

★ What discourages you most about the Christian life?

★ Do you know how patient God is with you? Do you understand that growing as a Christian is a process, not an unattainable destination?